Approaches to Communication Through Music

Approaches to Communication Through Music

MARGARET CORKE

with a Foreword from Dave Hewett

David Fulton Publishers

London

David Fulton Publishers Ltd
Ormond House, 26–27 Boswell Street, London WC1N 3JZ

First published in Great Britain by David Fulton Publishers in 2002

Note: The right of Margaret Corke to be identified as the author of this work has been asserted by her in accordance with the Copyright, Designs and Patents Act 1988.

Copyright © Margaret Corke 2002

British Library Cataloguing in Publication Data
A catalogue record for this book is available from the British Library.

ISBN 1-85346-843-6

Typeset by Kenneth Burnley, Wirral, Cheshire
Printed and bound in Great Britain by Bell and Bain Ltd, Glasgow

Contents

Foreword

What type of colleagues do you like to have around you for our work? Do you like them to be deeply committed, dedicated, thoughtful, reflective, knowledgeable and questioning? Do you have a preference for them being passionate and showing it, displaying emotions even – especially in their dissatisfaction with the lack of knowledge and technique that we all still have, in our work with people who have severe learning difficulties?

What kind of books do you want to read about our work? Do you have a preference for them to combine the detail of practice and description of the theories underpinning it? Books written in a user-friendly, accessible style? Perhaps books written by a dedicated practitioner who fits the description in the paragraph above? Somebody who has also studied their practice, read widely, furthered and developed it and then taken on the massive task of sharing their knowledge and experience with you in the written word?

If those things are what you want, congratulations – you have come to the right place. Read this book. You do not need to be a musician or to know about music to benefit from it. Having read it, you will know much more about how to help people who do not easily communicate and relate.

I have known Margaret Corke for a long time. Her school showed an early interest in Intensive Interaction, being concerned better to meet the needs of their more 'difficult to reach' students. Since that first contact more than 11 years ago, a core group of staff maintained their work on the development of approaches to teaching communication abilities to young people for whom this area is the priority concern. They have also maintained contact with me during this time, resulting in previous publication collaboration. The group of staff have been a stronghold for thought and development on interactive approaches to teaching.

Five years ago Margaret gave me a privately produced, spiral-bound book she had prepared with a colleague. It was entitled *Developing Interactive Music*. It described the development of what you will find in these pages. When I give courses, I put out tables at the back with books about our work, ones I believe are useful. Margaret's photocopied book is always on it, and it provokes more comment than any other publications, particularly, 'Where can I get a copy of this book?' I would tell them, and ultimately, I think, Margaret became bored with producing more copies for people and succumbed to the doom of writing for publication.

Reader, beware! This book might infect you with Margaret's zeal and passion. You may in turn become a truly reflective practitioner and commence the development of approaches, resulting in your own, brand new ideas for teaching things to people. You may then feel that what you have developed is good, vital even, and you must communicate it to other practitioners. You will now share Margaret's doom of the work involved in writing a book. She has made her very soul perspire in order to complete what she is sharing with you, and I think her soul is visible in the text.

Margaret's intensity and enthusiasm have me laughing frequently. I like my colleagues to be intense; I like them first and foremost to care deeply for the needs and lives of the people for whom we are working. I know that the quality of life of many people will be enhanced because of the existence of this book.

DAVE HEWETT
July 2001

Preface

The National Centre for Young People with Epilepsy (NCYPE) is the major provider of specialised services for young people with epilepsy in the UK.

Teamwork among a range of professionals – medical consultants, teachers, nurses, therapists, psychologists and skilled support staff – is the centrepiece of the NCYPE philosophy. Together, the teams support the special needs of students to achieve their true potential.

We are delighted to have the expert support of Margaret Corke, author of *Approaches to Communication Through Music*. Margaret is a key member of Clinical Services, working as an Interactive Music Specialist at NCYPE.

For further information about NCYPE please visit our website: *www.ncype.org.uk*, or telephone 01342 831237.

Acknowledgements

This manual would not have been written without the support and encouragement of my husband, Eric.

The approach owes much to the support, thoughts and ideas of others. Thank you to:

Valerie Stothard – I highly value her contribution, in both reading earlier drafts and redirecting me whenever I got lost. Her personal philosophy and insightful mind continuously guide my thinking.

Wendy Preveezer, whose course, 'Developing Communication Through Music', inspired the development of Interactive Music.

Dave Hewett, for his encouragement over many years, for reading my final draft(s) and, especially, for writing the Foreword to this book.

Sandy Turner, for her enthusiastic support and hard work assisting with the pilot study.

Jenny Terry, Katherine Wilshire, Michelle Patterson, Emma Tingley, Penny Pell, Ellen Laidler, Isabel Pine, Regeena Wright and *Julie Howlett*, with whom I have worked and from whom I have learned a great deal.

Father James Cutts, for insisting that I learn to play the guitar in the late 1980s, and *Father Aiden Murray*, for his spiritual guidance, for always believing in my academic abilities, even when I didn't, and for proofreading my final draft.

David Noyce, who so willingly and eloquently produced the music score for this book.

Mary and Joseph Loftus, my parents, for their love and encouragement always.

Chris Davies and *Rod Davies*, for their support and for giving me the opportunity to share Interactive Music with young people at St Piers, Lingfield.

And, especially, all the young people, classroom assistants and teachers with whom I have worked over many years. Their enthusiasm has enabled the approach to flourish. Because of them, others will now benefit.

Introduction

This manual reflects the development of my practice over many years and aims to make available to teachers, carers, parents and therapists the basic information required when sharing Interactive Music with people who have severe or profound and multiple learning difficulties. Tried and tested approaches and activities that help to promote communication and social interaction at a fundamental level will be put forward. Specialist and non-specialist alike, professional, parent or friend can use the simple songs, games and activities suggested. The greatest requisite is a willingness to interact in a positive, empathetic and sensitive manner.

In 1993, inspired by the work of Melanie Nind and Dave Hewett and a speech and language therapist, Wendy Preveezer, working in Nottingham (teaching a course on musical interaction), I began to develop Interactive Music, an approach devised to teach communication and social skills to people who are at an early developmental level. In particular, it has been helpful in developing the fundamental communication skills of those with severe or profound learning difficulties, including those with Autistic Spectrum Disorder.

The project led me on a learning journey, one that was to break through educational and therapeutic boundaries. Here, I strive to share the process and product with you. Without any real sense of direction, but with a burning desire to 'reach' those I worked with, I began to try out creative ideas and develop interactive activities.

Many of those with whom I now work fall into the lower ability spectrum wherein all areas of cognition and language are likely to be severely affected. People with additional neurological difficulties (damage to the brain resulting in non-functioning areas of the brain) or communication disorders such as autism are also on my caseload, and these present additional difficulties in terms of teaching and learning.

Looking back to the early 1990s, however, I had little understanding of a learner's 'condition' or developmental level – I just knew I liked being with them. Some appeared 'closed' and socially isolated. There were others, too, uniquely mischievous, clever problem-solvers, and those who were loud and gregarious. Some had a fighting spirit to match that of Sparticus, while others were quiet and withdrawn, waiting always for 'you' to make the first move. I saw, too, that these learners were often handicapped more by the people trying to educate them than by their own disability.

Educators tended to look for behavioural approaches, and emphasis was placed on programmes that were systematic and based on developing life skills. A hand-over-hand method of teaching was widely adopted and, sadly, this led to too much over-prompting. These were not bad days, merely special education in its infancy.

After all, it was not until the 1971 Education Act that students with severe learning difficulties were formally included in the education system.

In the early 1990s, when I first heard of Intensive Interaction (Nind and Hewett 1994), I knew I had found what I had been looking for. Their work changed my life. Its humanistic philosophy matched that of my own, and the approach, at last, seemed to consider the individuality and capability of learners.

I already loved music, but this also often seemed inaccessible to learners in the lower ability spectrum for whom weekly music sessions meant sitting in a circle, without being able to take an active part, except perhaps on an auditory level. Hand-over-hand prompts were used to 'help' learners play instruments and encourage participation. Many learners were pre-verbal, some pre-intentional (Coupe and Goldbart 1992); the one thing they most certainly had in common was their inability to sing, at least in the formal sense of the word. So songs were sung with gusto by staff, learners' arms were moved up and down, in and out, etc., according to the words of action songs. Often learners remained passive because of the inflexibility of an approach that was too fast-moving and unresponsive to their signals. Although many enjoyed the musical content, clearly their active input was minimal. Music, one of the most motivating sources for people with learning difficulties, was not being used to maximise their learning.

In search of a better way, I attended a course on musical interaction led by Wendy Preveezer. Her ideas and the way she linked these with Intensive Interaction were inspirational beyond words. She was a speech and language therapist who understood about fundamental communication. I hung on her every word. I knew this was the way forward.

The songs and activities that I then began writing seemed to work remarkably well. They engaged learners and moved them on interactively. As time went on, I realised I was on to something; something so simple it could be harnessed and used by many to support social interaction development at a fundamental level. The process, as it began to unfold, enabled me to make profound and meaningful connections with those I so desperately wanted to help. By following the interactive model adopted during Intensive Interaction (Nind and Hewett 1994) learners were enabled to be active in the learning process; to direct, control and develop the process by the way they responded. I used their ideas to mould and reshape my songs and activities.

As the value of Interactive Music became more evident, so, too, it became obvious that a practical idea may well be interesting, novel and successful, but if it lacks a sound knowledge base and firm theoretical perspective it also lacks credibility. I began to read (I had not read books for 20 years), listen to other professionals, attend relevant courses and, importantly, reflect upon and analyse my own professional practice. I developed an insatiable appetite for knowledge (culminating in a Bachelor of Arts degree) in the search of this thing I had called Interactive Music.

I met people who were to influence my attitude and creative thinking for ever. Naomi, a beautiful storyteller, was, at that time, working in children's theatre. Her manner was sincere and gentle, her style gracious and all-embracing. She weaved a magic web of stories that entranced adults and children alike. Her magic was made all the more tangible by her many props: old, well-travelled suitcases, a hat covered in story badges from around the world, unusual instruments from foreign lands, puppets, colour, surprise – and much more. She taught me, somewhat unwittingly, a great deal about performance, intrigue, anticipation and sharing delight.

John Childs is a music specialist, whose inventiveness had him arrive at a weekend music course with everything but the kitchen sink! As he presented his workshop we were encouraged to make music with toilet rolls, tin cans, pipes acquired from building sites, knives and forks and, indeed, anything – and that's nearly everything – that makes a sound. He was inspirational, and since then, I, too, have become an inventor of novel 'musical' equipment.

There were others, too, like Nick Huckleberry Beak, who taught me about clowning, facial expression, body language and having fun.

I learned from those who used 'wafting' sari material, stretchy lycra and all manner of materials during dance and movement work. I was on a mission, a mission that I hoped would change the often dreary lives of those people who find themselves at an early developmental level and who are trying to cope with a world that treats them too much like adults (way above their developmental level) and less like individuals.

The sensory curriculum (Longhorn 1988) also played its part in changing the way I thought. Its rationale provided meaningful insight into developmental education and transformed our understanding of 'special' curriculum. Essentially, however, Intensive Interaction remained at the heart of what I was doing. My task, it became clear over time, was to marry the two (creative and interactive) and, in doing so, provide a social learning environment that learners would want to be part of. These were exciting times of new discovery and development, and I journeyed with some very special people.

Valerie Stothard (1998) was one of these; she was also a pioneer in developing interactive strategies and techniques. It was she who challenged and nurtured me every step of the way. Indeed, we challenged each other, and in doing so, continually evaluated and reinvented what we were doing. This I believe to be one of the most important elements of good practice. Unless we are willing to be challenged, to learn from others, to learn from our mistakes and continually to re-evaluate our practice, we remain closed to new ideas and fail to grow.

This manual will serve as a practical guide for those who seek to establish developmental group work within their particular setting. Please note, however, that Interactive Music activities can be used in a variety of settings, including one-to-one (focused interaction aimed at building relationships and developing fundamental communication skills), two-to-one (encouraging peer interaction) and, as indicated, within group work (developing social language and communication skills).

The songs and activities could usefully be included as part of the early-years curriculum in mainstream education. Here emphasis could be placed on learning outcomes in literacy and numeracy.

Music, as the title suggests, is key to the approach but I wish to state quite clearly that Interactive Music can and has been successfully undertaken by the non-music professional and music professional alike. The songs are simple and, though guitar accompaniment can be really helpful, it is by no means essential. All the different elements together make Interactive Music what it is.

In an attempt to make this manual accessible to all professionals and disciplines

I have adopted the terms 'facilitator', 'helper' and 'learner' in order to identify and make clear specific roles inherent in the process.

This manual has been crafted in order to help the reader develop a better understanding of fundamental communication and a greater awareness of the personal and educational needs of learners who present as developmentally young. A sound knowledge base needs to be established before attempts are made to use the musical activities and game routines contained within this book.

Chapter 1 takes the reader through the approach and provides a gentle theoretical framework. The aims lay the foundations for the approach; the materials tell you what you need to deliver Interactive Music. The structure explains how and why Interactive Music is delivered, and finally the method provides readers with the nitty-gritty elements of performance and delivery.

Chapter 2 develops an understanding of the wider needs of learners – how each facet of their personhood can be embraced during the Interactive Music process. In a deliberate attempt to reflect the positive philosophy of the approach, helping words (enabling, valuing, nurturing, creating, encouraging and developing) introduce each specific area of development.

Chapter 3 contains the activities and cautions the reader not to use the activities for the activities' sake. To be powerful and effective the Interactive Music approach needs to be understood as a whole.

My earnest hope is that those who read this manual will become thoroughly imbued with its spirit and philosophy, and that this in turn will help them to develop the communication ability of those with whom they live or work.

To request information regarding training or to purchase Interactive Music CDs and tapes please write to: Margaret Corke, 55 Selsfield Road, Turners Hill, Nr Crawley, West Sussex, RH10 4PS, or e-mail: margaret.corke@ukonline.co.uk

1 The Approach

When working with those who have little or no speech, or limited comprehension of language, one of the ways forward is to use music. Engaging people both physically and emotionally, music impacts on mind, body and spirit. Within the Interactive Music process other components, namely fun, and visual, tactile and essentially person-centred approaches, combine with music to form the basis of a therapeutic approach devised to teach fundamental communication and social interaction.

Developmental research over the past few decades has provided an impressive body of information, particularly in relation to language and communication, and it is this that enables us to consider learning at its earliest. Throughout this manual I have drawn parallels between early infant development and the development of learners with profound or severe learning difficulties. While there are differences, much can be learned.

This chapter aims both to explain the nature of Interactive Music and to provide a gentle theoretical framework to underpin the approach.

Aims

The need to establish foundational skills before insisting on other attainments is paramount. In human terms, learning about social interaction must come first, but cognitive skills can be fostered during the communication learning process also. Skills, when learned, will need to be reinforced and consolidated for some time before other, more complex strategies can be acquired. This book will help guide readers through some of the pitfalls of teaching and suggest tried and tested developmental teaching strategies.

Any education process/programme should ensure that people who are unable to acquire even the most basic rudiments of spoken language are given an equal opportunity to develop alternative means of communication. This surely is a basic human right. Learners with profound, severe or complex and multiple learning difficulties will most definitely benefit from a curriculum where the emphasis is placed on using interactive approaches (Nind 1999).

Teaching must go at a pace learners can cope with and essentially educators must learn to recognise and adapt to learners' developmental level. In order to teach the rudiments of social interaction and communication we must start from basics and ensure that learners are ready and able to move on to the next stage. Only when firm foundations are laid can progress ensue. This makes perfect sense to me, but I continue to see practitioners striving to teach the seemingly unattainable. Let me try to get my point across by using a hypothetical case study:

Rory is a ten-year-old boy, functioning within Piaget's (1952) 'sensory motor' stage of development. He has complex and multiple learning difficulties compounded by a severe neurological condition. Rory has difficulty understanding and using facial expression and gestures. He has no apparent means of asking for what he wants, and more often than not is helped with everything he does. His behaviour is considered to be pre-intentional.

Rory presents multiple challenges to educators who must provide him with a 'needs relevant' curriculum but 'within the letter of collective policy demands' (Clough 1998). This, as Clough explains, causes tension both pedagogically and in terms of teacher role. As an example he notes tension between 'the needs of the student' and the demands of the law. The notion of 'curriculum for all' was thrust upon special schools in the Education Reform Act (1988). Whether or not it included any consideration of the cognitive and social ability of 'special' students is debatable.

In general, then, it seems to me that teachers in this field are left to manage key curriculum areas such as English and mathematics, with little or no knowledge of developmental research or any idea of the wealth of information it could provide to inform their work. Instead, I have observed that many continue to adopt skill acquisition exercises beyond the cognitive level of students. For example, imagine trying to 'help' Rory (hand over hand) to hold a pencil in order to write his name, or physically hold on to his thumb during the 'Hello' song as if it were his greeting. This is nonsensical. Why? Well, put yourself in Rory's shoes; what is he learning from these experiences? Perhaps, sadly, only how uncomfortable it feels to have a hand grasped by a stronger person. Cognitively he has not yet reached a stage where he even understands object concept (what an object is), let alone the value of the written word or what a pencil can do. Rory needs to go back to the beginning, back to basics. He has a right to an education that meets his needs and improves his quality of life. Were I to be in his position, perhaps I might develop behaviours (say biting my hand or spitting) in order to avoid doing the task. Need I say more?

The aims listed below are fundamental to all learning. Key learning areas are identified and this provides a foundational framework for social and cognitive learning at a basic level. Each aim, when achieved, will help to provide a cornerstone for subsequent learning.

- To have fun and to develop an inner satisfaction at communicating effectively.
- To tolerate the closeness of another person.
- To enjoy being with another person.
- To initiate and maintain social interaction.
- To develop and understand early communication, such as meaningful eye contact, body language, facial expression, anticipation and turn-taking exchanges.
- To develop sound production and vocal imitation skills.
- To explore and understand the given physical environment, including instruments and sound-making items.
- To develop an understanding of cause and effect, both socially (how their behaviour affects others) and physically (how their behaviour affects their environment).
- To develop physical imitation skills.

- To develop extended 'conversation', using a combination of the above skills, together with any language the student may possess, meaningful or otherwise.
- To develop self-esteem from knowing that the person interacting with them is also enjoying the interaction, i.e. they want to be there.
- To express and develop a sense of their own feelings

Materials

Us – face, body language and voice

Without a doubt the most important pieces of learning equipment, readily available, are our face, body and voice. It is we and we alone who have the power to change the interactive potential of those with whom we work. Indeed it could be hypothesised that a learner's success as a potential communicator depends upon how much exposure they have to quality human interaction. We turn to the 'moves' of primary caregivers to gain insight into what quality interaction may involve. Research has shown that, in developmental terms, caregivers prove to be our best 'teachers'. Stern (1977) notes that a mother, when interacting with her infant, spends a great deal of time '. . . playing the natural instruments of her voice, face and body and orchestrating them for and in conjunction with her baby', who in turn becomes 'affectively alive'. This surely is just what we hope for during interaction – that our learners become affectively alive. Stern further describes the mother's behaviour as the best 'sound and light show on earth'. All this from one human being to another and simply arising out of an innate ability to 'tune in' to others at an emotional level.

Essentially, learners must be enabled to become active partners in the process. Our exaggerated facial expression and expectant body language hold every possibility of drawing out a reluctant 'speaker'. Giving lots of time, using expectant pauses, providing listener feedback and essentially exuding non-verbal messages like, 'Come on then, I'm listening' or 'I'm here, ready and waiting, it's up to you now – I am listening with my heart as well as my face' prove far more powerful than using verbal or physical prompts.

Pease (1993) notes that researchers such as Albert Mehrabian (1969, 1971) found that the total impact of a message is about 7 per cent verbal, 38 per cent vocal and 55 per cent non-verbal. Thus what 'really' happens between interactive partners happens without many words at all. Our body and face in particular provide a mobile stimulus that is continually signalling, often changing and always communicating whether we are aware of it or not. The non-verbal messages we give are likely to be far more powerful than anything we might say.

The voice, too, in all its guises, adds to the free flow of interactions. 'No matter how important lexico-grammatical meaning eventually becomes, the human brain is first organised or programmed to respond to emotional/intonational aspects of the human voice' (Dissanayake 1990 in Storr 1992:9). Our attention is drawn to 'motherese', a universal 'vowel drenched' speaking style (Kuhl and Meltzoff 1997). They note that this is socially pleasing for the infant, both holding its attention and focusing the infant on the talking adult. The interchange between mothers and infants contains elements of metre, rhythm, pitch, volume and lengthening of vowel sounds. It is no wonder then that musical capabilities are seen in infants before linguistic ones (Slobada 1996 in Lowis 1998). The power so evident within the human voice could usefully be harnessed and used in creative ways during episodes of interaction. Music, even in its most basic form, holds a kind of 'magic' that can be all-embracing. You don't need to be a good singer, just a good communicator who is willing to explore and experiment vocally.

Detailed analysis of infant–caregiver behaviour during face-to-face encounters has enabled a greater understanding of the subtle cues that invite, modulate and terminate everyday interactions (Stern 1977). List (1963 in Wood 1992) argues that within everyday interactions a system of visual signals occurs between people. Such findings, says Wood (1973:146), imply that the 'tuning in' of speakers and listeners is rooted in some shared biological rhythmic system. This, he further explains, accounts for the possibility of universal synchronisation of mutual movement where unconscious aspects of non-verbal communication effect interaction between partners. We cannot assume learners are reading our unconscious messages, therefore we must constantly monitor our own behaviour while earnestly 'reading' theirs. Whether negative or reinforcing, our behaviour can have a huge effect on the interactive performance of learners.

Each person will develop their own particular interactive style dependent upon personality and personal characteristics. 'Emotional expressiveness, speed of movement, responsiveness, tenseness, playfulness – these and many other personality attributes differentiate people and help to produce distinctive interactive style' (Nind 2000b).

Both partners bring to the interchange their inbred temperamental characteristics, but essentially the facilitator, as more able partner, needs to adjust his or her behaviour in order first to acknowledge the learner's behaviour. Facilitators, too, need to think about the way they communicate in order to be able to acknowledge the learner's behaviour. Facilitators also need to think about and take into account the learner's understanding of non-verbal communication. Face-to-face interaction, synchrony, turn-taking, reciprocal vocalisation and shared emotional states are seen to be characteristic forms of caregiver–infant interactions (Schaffer 1998).

We need to be constantly ready and open for interaction and ready also to use our face, body and voice to reinforce positively the learner, to convey acceptance, patience and a desire to communicate at the learner's level. Reinforcing head-nods, a face that is full of delight and a look of expectancy can trigger a response from a reluctant 'speaker': the kind of non-verbal message that says, 'Yeah, go on then, I really want to listen to you.'

Social interaction game routines

> The study of social development refers to the behaviour patterns, feelings, attitudes and concepts manifest in relation to other people. (Schaffer 1998:1)

In this statement Schaffer embraces the fundamental nature of human interaction, acknowledging that without verbal understanding, elementary social connections are being made. Interactive Music seeks to develop learners' competence in understanding and managing interpersonal relationships, enabling them to become sociable, friendly and companionable. Fundamental communication strategies, when learned, will support this. Adopting categories of parent–child interactions, both social and didactic, proves to be significant. The social mode refers to physical and verbal strategies adopted during interpersonal exchanges, whereas the didactic method refers to stimulating and arousing by encouraging attention to objects or events in the environment (Bornstein 1983 in Gleason 1989). Each of these modes contributes towards the Interactive Music process.

Making sense of encounters with people helps learners to develop an understanding of their experience within interpersonal situations.

> Children must develop powers of recognising and sharing emotional states, of interpreting and anticipating others' reactions, of understanding the relationships between others, of comprehending the sanctions, prohibitions and accepted practices of their world. (Dunn 1988:5)

This is by no means an easy task for learners with complex and multiple learning difficulties who may show neither the will nor the ability to interact. Here Nind and Hewett (1994) favour 'process teaching', suggesting that social learning cannot be undertaken coldly from a professional-seeming distance. Based on the model of caregiver–infant interaction their approach (Intensive Interaction) is humanistic and respectful. It works! Evaluation of its effectiveness concludes that not only does it add to quality of life but it also helps pupils to learn and apply new skills (Watson and Knight 1991; Nind 1996; Watson and Fisher 1997 in Nind 1999).

Once again the natural model of development informs our thinking and gives us a greater understanding of how learning takes place. Individuals participating in joint interactive activities learn about the to-and-fro of social interaction. In play, game routines prove useful not only for the pleasure they cause but because 'they are conventional, oft-repeated routines requiring the mutual involvement of the two participants and are based on clear rules, of which turn-taking and repetition of rounds are most common' (Schaffer 1998).

At a pre-verbal level, game routines are likely to have profound implications for social and cognitive development. Anticipation games, such as 'Here I come – got you', offer educators a means for developing cognition. 'Practical intelligence takes the form of anticipating a state of affairs' (Wood 1992:20); if a child can imagine and anticipate a particular consequence, then it is likely that they are able to 'hold or represent what is sought in mind' (Wood 1992). Peek-a-boo games give pleasure and intensify social interactive episodes; again there is an element of expecting the unexpected and a means for developing cognition. Games involving give and take can help establish basic conversational rules such as turn-taking and extend opportunities for 'topic sharing' (infant–object–adult situations) (Schaffer 1998).

Nind and Hewett (1994) urge adults to find playfulness within themselves and to use it carefully and thoughtfully in their work. Games need to be enjoyable, socially rewarding and fun. 'The fundamental importance of mutual involvement and mutual pleasure has also been illustrated, this creating the motivation for both parties to repeat and develop interactive games' (Bromwich 1981; Hodapp and Goldfield 1983 in Nind 1996).

Within the context of Interactive Music, activities which are offered as part of each particular game routine provide input, individually or collectively, via all the sensory channels. Wester (1991) has intimated that: 'repetitious auditory input such as singing or rhyming, visual distraction with toys or presentation of a familiar toy to hold' can offer a means of hypnotic intervention for those at a sensory motor stage of development. I am not suggesting that Interactive Music hypnotises learners, merely that sessions can be all-embracing and helpful in maintaining learners' focus. As well as providing learners with an incentive to communicate, social interactive game routines aim to make learners aware of their external environment, to provide opportunities for problem-solving and to nurture a learner's sense of well-being. In order to communicate intentionally a child must want to communicate, have something to communicate about, have someone to communicate with and realise that communication is enjoyable and can bring results (Coupe and Goldbart 1992).

Game strategies

Burst-pause

A burst can be physical, jiggling or rocking or a verbal/sung phrase. A pause can be still and silent, expectant in nature (gasp/facial expression) or playful (exaggerated facial expression). Within the pause the learners signal a desire to continue by whatever means they possess. Learners fill the pause with an appropriate signal phrase, word, sound or gesture.

Anticipation

Anticipation games should be repetitive in nature and contain a dramatic build-up (possibly using rising intonation) before the anticipated outcome is realised. During the build-up you will be looking for a particular communicative response dependent on the developmental level of the learner. Here the facilitator's expectant body language and facial expression encourage an appropriate response.

Rough and tumble

Rough and tumble games such as 'Push and Pull', 'Tumbling' and 'Jiggling' contain bois-terous physical elements. They may be useful for raising arousal levels. During such games we must be sensitive to the likes and dislikes of learners. These games should be repetitive and may include elements of burst-pause and anticipation.

Give and take

Give and take games can establish basic conversational rules. These games need to be playful and learner led – only give and take when the learner is ready to relinquish objects willingly. In the first instance exchanging objects may be easier. Ball games, rolling cars, etc. can be incorporated into this category. Use key words like 'give' and lots of positive reinforcement.

Physical activities

Games that incorporate structured physical routines such as clapping or tickling hands, feet/toe games and rocking/rowing, etc. can be used to develop anticipation. Used con-sistently they can become part of a learner's repertoire. Nursery rhymes, poems and songs should be incorporated.

Hide and find – Peek-a-boo

Hats, scarves, fans, pieces of material and hands can all be used to hide and draw atten-tion to the face. These games will include elements of suspense and anticipation. Hide and find games offer a means of teaching object-permanence.

Back and forward

I have found this type of game especially useful where learners tend to want to throw things all the time. Tie a piece of ribbon or string to an object and when the learner pushes/throws it away, let it swing back to them so that they can push/throw it again, thus setting up a game routine. In my experience this eventually leads to greater exploration of objects. A ball, toy, car, etc. can of course also be rolled in a back-and-forth way.

Music

Music is scanned in the right-hand side of the brain, thus linking it with our emotions. Music appreciation requires no verbal understanding; it goes beyond intellect and therefore is accessible to all levels of intelligence. We can't be free from it, even if we so desire, notes Boethius (Storr 1992). Professor Paul Robinson (1996), too, points out that music, even in its most basic form, connects directly with our emotions and is uniquely involved with memory and personal identity. Further, he notes that even with profound neurological damage the musical personality remains. Importantly for us, learners can share musical experiences and communicate on many different levels in ways that require no words at all. Music, then, is vital because it intensifies the input, especially at an emotional level. It holds the whole group process of Interactive Music together.

Wendy Preveezer has written about the value of using musical interaction with children, and in particular those with autism:

> It can help to cue and mark alternating turns in conversational exchanges, emphasise rhythmic flow, create or enhance suspense and resolution, and bridge momentary gaps where the child's attention might otherwise be lost. (Preveezer 2000)

Musical Interaction Therapy (originally developed in Nottingham by staff at Sutherland House School) (Christie and Wimpory 1986) seeks to facilitate social interaction experiences between young children with autism and their carers. The approach has been validated by research (Wimpory 1995a; Wimpory 1995b; Wimpory and Nash 1999). The music specialist's role is specific to the approach (Preveezer 2000). Unlike music therapy, a direct relationship with the child through the music is not sought. Rather the specialist, using live music, facilitates and enhances interaction between carer and child by attending to every movement and action. Musical commentary complements and extends the interaction. 'Musical input often enables the interaction to go on longer and to develop in more intense and diverse ways' (Preveezer 2000).

Similarities can be drawn between Musical Interaction Therapy and Interactive Music. Both focus on developing social interaction game routines; both elicit and develop social interaction by using live accompanying music that enables flexibility and responsiveness towards learners' expressive movements and non-verbal signals. Unlike the Musical Interaction Therapist, however, the specialist using Interactive Music directly seeks to form a meaningful relationship with learners. This is not achieved exclusively through music but rather through a multi-sensory approach among which music and Intensive Interaction (Nind and Hewett 1994) are key players.

Distinctions, too, can be drawn between the roles of a Music Therapist and an Interactive Music Specialist. It is likely that each particular discipline uses sounds and music to nurture a relationship between learner and 'therapist' in order to '. . . encourage physical, mental, social and emotional well-being' (Bunt 1994) but the Interactive Music Specialist also seeks directly and purposefully to develop play, sensory exploration, motor skills and a learner's ability to communicate. The framework is structured, the process person-centred; simple songs, activities and social game routines are incorporated, and bizarre and novel items are used alongside instruments to gain and maintain attention.

The approach is very simple and can be undertaken by specialist and non-specialist alike – parent, teacher or friend. Used creatively, songs and activities can be suitably integrated into every aspect of the special curriculum or used at home during 'special times' with parents or friends to nurture positive relationships. Versatility and the fact that you don't have to be musical or qualified to share Interactive Music help to make it unique.

Interactive Music can be presented within a range of settings but its strength may lie in the fact that it works well when used in a group setting. 'Music has long been used as a means of expressing both group and personal identity' (Bunt 1994). A group provides opportunities for social learning in a 'real' social setting. Music provides a backdrop that is both pleasing and cohesive. As Storr (1992) explains, ' . . . it has the effect of underlining the emotions which a particular event calls forth by simultaneously co-ordinating the emotions of a particular group of people'.

Olds' (1985) study is fascinating, suggesting innate musical origins, it seems to me, with internal body rhythms and the 'spirit of the person'. Olds (1985) found that from 25 weeks the foetus not only hears music but also responds and interacts with it. Foetal response also indicated an ability to differentiate between different kinds of music and then to display likes and dislikes. In the same vein Storr (1992) suggests that perhaps 'auditory perception prompts the baby's first realisation that there is something beyond itself'. Could music, as Dissangale (1990 in Storr 1992) argues, have originated in verbal exchanges between mother and baby? If so, how much more likely is it that music awakens the interest, both physical and emotional, of those who are developmentally young?

So singing, or at least using one's voice in an interesting way, holds possibilities for gaining attention. When we sing we tend to become more interesting, not necessarily because of our beautiful singing voice, but because as we sing our facial expression, body language and voice patterns tend to change.

Multi-sensory

Effective educational outcomes can be achieved when the interest and skill of learners is recognised and considered during educational planning. When the developmental level is low, starting from the learner's frame of reference generally means starting at a sensory level. Sensory input provides learners with experiences that enable them to access information about themselves, their world and the people in their world. The sensory nature of the activities provides learners with a range of experiences and a means of reaching them on many different levels. Activities often help to build bridges between facilitators, helpers and learners, and, as Longhorn (2000) says: 'The senses breach the barrier into the world of special people.'

Activity items used during Interactive Music sessions are often bright, colourful, novel and interesting – things that attract attention and arouse interest. With such a wide range of materials being presented, care needs to be taken to ensure that stimulation does not prove confusing and consequently counterproductive. In early childhood the mother finds a balance, protecting against excessive dosages of stimulation as well as supplying extra stimuli, thereby helping to modulate the infant's general arousal level (Schaffer 1971). Getting the balance just right may be difficult and involves trial and error on both sides. Sensitivity and selectivity, according to student response, informs our choice and guides our delivery.

Music is vital to the approach because it intensifies input at an emotional level; it holds the whole thing together. During sessions sensory input is purposefully upped so that all sensory channels, as far as possible, are awakened. This helps learners to develop a repertoire of actions; they are challenged on many levels and gently guided toward active exploration. 'Pointing out, reminding, suggesting and praising all serve to orchestrate and structure the child's activities under the guidance of one who is more expert' (Wood 1998:98).

Guide to sensory exploration

It is important to consider the stages of sensory exploration. Most learners will actually have a preferred way of learning about people and their world. For example, I have worked with an autistic boy who likes to stand up and drop items to the floor; he then rocks profusely, watching all the time until he decides to retrieve, shake and once again drop it on the floor. During this process he has felt it, explored its properties and observed it – I applaud it as a means of exploration. The worst scenario for a lad like this would be to encourage him, using hand-over-hand prompts; to explore items according to some fixed idea of how it should be done.

When offering sensory experiences, environmental or social, we need to start from a learner's frame of reference – what the learner can and wants to do. This means observing learners for long enough to know how best he or she can independently access the materials being presented, and in particular how the learner chooses to explore. One might, for example, present a drum for the learner to bang – a subtle signal from the learner, however, might inform us of their need to feel the drum up close to the face. This may, for that particular learner, be the best way actually to receive sensory input.

Many learners, too, will like to mouth objects in order to learn about their properties. Learners should be allowed to use their ideas and be given opportunities to learn by trial and error.

The way we present activities, and our empathetic response to the way learners choose to explore, guides our thinking. Importantly, getting the pace 'right' for each individual is vital. All too often there is a temptation to offer 'experience' for the sake of the curriculum. A sensory approach to the curriculum now tends to have superseded the 'sensory curriculum' (Davis 2001). Here, sensory learning is encouraged naturally throughout the day.

Many teachers rely on sensory elements to teach a variety of subjects including topic-related theme work. This is helpful, and especially so when the materials are presented empathetically. Learners' lives will certainly be enriched by such experiences, but great care needs to be taken to ensure learners are 'really' participating and understanding, and not just experiencing by having things done to them by more able partners.

During Interactive Music sessions, great care needs to be taken when presenting materials, and the facilitator's responses and awareness of individuals' exploratory levels need to be taken into account. Importantly, the process should be learner-led. The facilitator needs to be totally flexible. If a learner requires more time to explore, ensure this happens. The facilitator can choose to move on to the next activity so that others are not kept waiting for too long. This tends to be a bit of a balancing act but well worth the effort in terms of leaner empowerment and overall participation.

Stages of sensory exploration

- *Just being* – learning to accept and tolerate their world. (Passive and seemingly unresponsive.)
- *Slight awareness* – reflex responses, eye movements, head-turning, subtle body movements.
- *Limited awareness* – positive or negative (facial expression and body language signals) reaction to environment and stimuli. (Turns away, pushes or pulls away, turns towards.)
- *Some awareness* – responsive, glances, watching. Holding but often dropping objects. Hand–mouth coordination, tracking. (Mouths objects, holds objects, tentative exploration.)
- *Awareness developing* – attentive, engages in exploration at a simple level. Reach gesture, holds and mouths objects, range of responses increases. Inconsistent responses to anticipation games. Pays increasing attention to favoured objects. (Tactile exploration, manipulation, investigation.)
- *Developing* – purposeful, hand–eye coordination, extended exploration, awareness of cause and effect. May use a person's hand as a tool to access stimuli. Learners will want to repeat experiences they have particularly liked. Anticipates outcomes. (Shakes objects, hits objects against nearby surfaces, bangs a drum with hands.)
- *Extending* – developing a range of responses and various new means to achieve specific outcomes. Object concept developing – aware of size, shape, properties and functions of objects.

- *Experimenting.* (Appropriate use of objects. Examines, throws and follows with eyes, bangs two objects together, problem-solving, bangs drum with beater, holds and bangs two cymbals, etc.)

Facilitators and helpers need to be sensitive to each individual and enable them to access stimuli (activity items) at an appropriate level. Where the ability level is very low, a slow pace is most appropriate. Learners at this level often require a lot of time to formulate a response.

Remember, it is not enough to offer learners sensory experiences. Learners are encouraged to be active participants in the learning process. At all levels learners are invited to direct, control and lead, by using whatever means they possess. **Presenting learners with experiences to which they have no active input actually ignores their ability and does little or nothing to nurture their development.**

Structure

Structure/process

Although the process is person-centred, the framework is structured. There is a ritual, a routine and a perception of what's going to happen. The sequence of events and the components, such as melodies and rewards, are known. During sessions positive reinforcement is used to encourage appropriate communicative responses and social behaviours. Importantly, the process adopts a humanistic person-centred philosophy attributed to Rogers (1961) wherein four core conditions – empathy, warmth, unconditional positive regard and congruence – help to foster positive relationships. Negative reinforcement is not advocated. Extinction techniques are used in an attempt to eliminate particularly unhelpful behaviours. This involves ignoring the behaviour and thus not reinforcing it. Behaviour shaping also plays its part. Here, successive approximations towards a desired behaviour are reinforced through an appropriate reward, generally of a social nature. Challenging behaviours, with some creative thinking, can at times be shaped into something more appropriate by distracting learners through the use of playful strategies. Importantly, although the facilitator acts on directly observable behaviour, he or she considers psychological processes and the emphasis remains person-centred.

In adopting a person-centred approach, Interactive Music requires facilitators and helpers to treat learners as equal; really to understand their feelings; to join them in their 'conversations'; to follow their line of regard and, through positive use of body language, tone of voice and musical expression, to convey understanding and empathy. When this occurs, learners progress, through their increasing openness to social, physical and environmental experience. Feelings of being dominated or threatened seem to subside and mutual trust is established.

A positive structured framework creates a 'safe', contained, predictable and secure space. The person-centred approach means that the facilitator supports learning at the appropriate developmental level, in a way that reaches deeply and impacts more.

So, in many ways the agenda is a shared one. The facilitator delivers the activities but learners, at any time, can change that agenda by the way they act or behave. The content of a session is informed as much by the learner's actions as the facilitator's planning. 'The teacher's style and role becomes one of enabling students to become active in their own learning' (Collis and Lacey 1996:9). As the facilitator responds contingently to the learner's signals and subtle spontaneous behaviours, learners are actively involved in the process and their ideas effect, mould and change the process. The facilitator, while actively considering communication objectives, remains flexible in order to go with the learner's interactive 'flow'. One of the challenges within this process, as Nind and Hewett (1994) point out, is to 'retain the power of intuitive responding whilst supplementing it with the benefits of careful analysis to maximise the potential of the interactions'.

Learners such as ours cannot easily cope with an open-ended scenario. They cannot predict or act outside a framework. If the framework is too flexible it can lead to anxiety and withdrawal. This Interactive Music approach provides a structured framework, thereby creating a 'safe', contained, predictable and secure space, which makes it easier for learners to open up. Let me try to explain. Consider an anticipation activity; for example, the facilitator chooses the game and prop (tickling stick). He or she initiates the game: 'Here I come, ready, steady . . .'; a pause, and within this pause the facilitator holds an expectation that the learner will respond in a certain way – perhaps, for example, eye contact, or reach, or pulling the prop toward themselves or saying 'Go', etc. An air of flexibility hangs within this expectation because in the end the facilitator accepts the learner's 'best' signal on any particular day. Thus, with each repetition of the activity the song (individual to each particular activity) is always the same and the prop is predetermined, causing the learner to feel safe and secure within this framework. The unexpected and unplanned-for aspects of the approach, and what make it person-centred, are in the outcomes. The facilitator gives time for a response and acts accordingly.

Essentially we must hold an expectation that learners will extend and develop their communication potential. When parents treat their infant's behaviour with intention, they treat them as 'understandable beings' (Stern 1977). The suggestion is that we treat learners as though they were roughly the person they are about to become (Vygotsky 1962).

Interaction and attachment

Clearly, for interaction to take place, two people are required and each must relate to the other. 'All learning and all creative acts begin in the domains of emergent relatedness' (Stern 1985). In the realms of Interactive Music, outcomes arise not merely because of the music, not especially because of the activity items but essentially because of the 'interactiveness' of the approach. Each week we, the group, meet; relationships flourish as more able partners acknowledge and respect learners' desires to communicate. Learners are listened to in the active, empathetic sense of the word, and over time meaningful connections are made. This is no one-way street; both partners have to want interaction (an emotional connection) before the attachment process can even begin to evolve. I now believe that this attachment happens because, as we come to know learners in adopting a responsive communicative style, so we experience 'what it's like to be you'; we act with understanding towards the other person and each, in turn, gains confidence in the other. 'Each person also has an inner face which is always sensed but never seen' (O'Donohue 1999:27). When trust is built a learner will respond, often in very subtle ways – they 'let you in' and you know it.

Game routines, especially those that are entirely interactive, help to nurture the attachment process. Here, activity items, presented with sensitivity, can build bridges between learner and helper. Music and playfulness, too, support the 'tuning in' process. They both affect our inner chemistry in a unique way. Shared with others, fun provides a means of intensifying affective experiences and creates opportunities for relationship building.

In the natural infant–caregiver model, the caregiver is seen to connect emotionally with the infant and it is this affect sharing that makes the interaction meaningful in human terms. Strict imitation of another person's actions alone is not enough. Stern (1985) notes that several processes have to take place:

> First, the parent must be able to read the infant's feeling state from the infant's overt behaviour. Second, the parent must perform some behaviour that is not strict imitation but nonetheless corresponds in some way to the infant's behaviour. Third, the infant must be able to read the corresponding parental response as having to do with the infant's own original feeling experience and not just imitating the infant's behaviour. (Stern 1985:139)

Providing close or loose imitation of a learner's behaviours may not be enough. Stern (1985:144) points to Mahler and Furer (1968); Kohut (1977); Lacan (1977), who note that reflecting back an infant's feeling state is important to the infant's developing knowledge of his or her own affectivity and sense of self. Affect attunement during infant–caregiver interaction is seen to happen almost automatically and this is just as likely to occur during our interaction with learners. Pure imitation alone (mirroring and echoing learners' behaviour) will not work. There has to be a commitment from both parties and an emotional connection made.

Bowlby (1969) has identified three fundamental principles of adaptive social behaviour: reciprocity, affectance and trust. Acquisition of these, as Craig (2000) explains, represents a significant milestone in the attachment process.

Conclusion

During Interactive Music sessions, the learning environment created seeks first to value the person and then to discover what motivates and interests them. Having observed and discovered this, the facilitator provides interactive musical/creative activities and games in order to elicit a communicative response and social interaction by capitalising on what intrigues and delights that individual. In all situations the approach celebrates what the person can do and then builds on individual talents, strengths and skills. This enables learners to find their social environment interesting and attractive as well as helping them to develop a sense of themselves in relation to others.

Undertaking specific musical activities in a group enables learners to display their interactive potential and practise social behaviour. This, I suggest, helps them to form social concepts. Activities include elements that help learners to organise and refine their behaviour towards others, as well as elements that develop an understanding of self. Learners display their interactive potential in the knowledge that it will be celebrated and acted upon.

Perhaps most importantly, Interactive Music aims to leave learners with a 'feel-good' factor. Anticipation games, interactive songs, sung/musical running commentary, improvisation and creative surprises combine in an environment where fun and laughter are commonplace. We rejoice and delight in the ability of these very special people.

Method

Group dynamics

We are all born into social groups of one form or another, and inevitably, over time, we will most likely be part of many different kinds of social groups. Indeed, as Forsyth (1999) notes, many of our waking hours are spent within settings consisting of groups. Roles, norms and other structural aspects of group life lie somewhat unnoticed but are in fact at the heart of most groups.

The learners for whom Interactive Music was originally devised fall into the category of some of the most challenging in terms of their ability and willingness to interact in social settings. They may not automatically seek social, group-orientated inclusion and some may even find group life an isolating and uncomfortable experience. Learners then may need help and empathetic understanding in order to connect with others socially. A group needs to be a place in which members feel safe and secure. Facilitator and helpers alike need to be sensitive to each individual's needs and flexible in accommodating them, otherwise social learning may not occur. Through association with others we can come to know and understand others.

> Our personal identity describes our unique idiosyncratic qualities, it is the 'me' component of the self. Our social identity describes our connections to other people, to groups, and to society; it is the 'we' component of self. (Forsyth 1999:70)

Inevitably, within a group, people who interact with each other influence each other. 'Any change in one induces a ripple effect in others' (Button 1985).

Group norms – growing expectation of what can and can't occur

Consideration needs to be given to the fact that behaviour by group members may have less to do with group norms and more to do with their cognitive ability or neurological conditions. Throughout the session, what more able partners do, say and how they react prove instrumental in helping learners to learn and conform to group norms. 'Certain behaviour is repeated, becomes normal and the expected thing and other members of the group adjust themselves to that expected behaviour' (Button 1985).

Group norms in our particular context are, for example, that learners sit on a chair in the circle. Leaving the circle usually means leaving the activities also. Group members seem to know that a particular song signals the beginning and end of a session. A contract exists in that I will be there for them at this time each week. Listening, waiting, interaction and turn-taking are encouraged, and conformity to these skills most likely ends in mutual satisfaction. Learners, too, know that their actions can effect and direct the process. As Wright (1987) suggests, 'Establish the early norms of freedom of communication, the open communication and feelings and style of listening which is alternative and non-critical.'

Roles – the part played or taken on within a group

We all play a role as part of a group. It is likely that we all have our own 'type' (the way we usually behave) but may choose to go in and out of role during the group life. Learners and helpers will hold distinct role types which can be identified after close observation. Learners, too, are likely to share common features with their more able partners. Within sessions, then, people may take on roles such as: enabler, helper, experimenter, dominator, obstructer, manipulator, follower, harmoniser, communicator, observer, participator, commentator and encourager, to name but a few.

The role played out by more able partners has a significant effect upon possible learning outcomes arising from sessions. Clearly, as has already been stressed, those who play positive roles contribute the most to positive outcomes. As an example, let us consider the role of 'helper', a positive role one might think – or is it? He or she is a first-rate helper but because he or she is so helpful, at times, he or she helps too much. Helpers often feel it is their job to be 'doing' when, in fact, it is the learner who should be 'doing'. An 'enabler' on the other hand will help, but not necessarily by doing; rather, by finding ways to enable the learners to succeed for themselves.

In order to consider the role played out by individuals in a group, it is helpful to step back and consider the roles people play. Ask yourself how best you can facilitate positive outcomes for learners.

Group setting

A group may indeed be a collection of individuals, but each, though unique, will affect and be affected by the behaviour of others within that group. I have noticed that although learners may appear to be unaware of others and may not display an ability to interact in a meaningful way, a connection is nevertheless often taking place.

The group gathers, usually weekly, and we sit in a circle; this helps the dynamics and interactions. A circle creates a sense of togetherness and equality; it feels safe and suggests a clear boundary; it is non-threatening and offers inclusion; it also signals that this time is special and different from the rest of the day.

The group process requires learners to understand that 'everyone is special, not just me'. Once mastered (not always easy), relationships can be fostered which lead to real social learning. A group holds many advantages, creating by its very nature opportunities for interaction, turn-taking, looking, listening, sharing, observing others, being the centre of attention and having fun. As each person's contribution or non-contribution is accepted and celebrated, the process has the potential of having a cohesive and therapeutic effect. Within this framework human interaction can be facilitated in a natural and spontaneous way. The attitude of the facilitator, the pace and structure of the session and the nature of the activities ensure a high level of attentiveness, interaction and achievement throughout.

Establishing and forming a group may take time. We have to come to know and accept each other's weaknesses and strengths, and for a long time learners and helpers may feel threatened or unsure. A routine needs to be established. The place, time and space will serve to form a contract, and the facilitator's positive attitude, actions and confidence will foster a positive feel within the group.

Equality will be established if those supporting take their turn alongside learners. This certainly proves helpful in uniting the group, but is particularly useful because it models to learners alternative ways to act or explore. Besides, it is good for us to share the same experiences and to feel what it's like to participate on many different levels. It is important to stress, however, that learners and helpers must always be given the opportunity to choose whether or not to participate. They can say or indicate 'No' to any particular activity. We need to respect their feelings at all times. Cajoling and persuasion from time to time may be necessary but this is always done with sensitivity – to encourage rather than insist.

Throughout the session, emotions and feelings may manifest themselves as behaviours. This can provide helpful information as to the feelings of group members. Assumptions of people's emotions and feelings, however, can be a risky business. We can attempt to read these signs and signals only by knowing the learners' histories and by watching on many occasions. Consideration also needs to be given to the fact that in certain situations, learners' behaviours and body language may be symptomatic of disability, disorder or brain damage. Becoming attuned to group members (whether facilitator learner or learner facilitator) takes time.

Group size

An Interactive Music group requires at least two learners plus helper/s. More than eight, in my experience, proves difficult simply because waiting time between turn-taking is too long. A group of six with helpers as required and a facilitator is ideal. You of course will know what is best for those you are trying to help. Larger groups may be suitable for more able learners.

Guidelines for facilitators

Empathy underpins all aspects of the Interactive Music approach. At all times and in all situations, we should put ourselves in the learner's shoes. Our response then can be guided by reflecting on our internal as well as external knowledge of the situation.

- The facilitator has a 'real' willingness to become a good communicator. Aspects of good communication are explained in the remaining bullet points.
- The facilitator has a working knowledge of and an ability to read communication signals.
- The facilitator ensures that the learning environment created is attractive, motivating, stimulating and, above all, interactive – no mean task!
- The facilitator possesses personality attributes such as sensitivity, honesty, responsiveness and a sense of fun.
- The facilitator displays an ability to listen actively, is intuitive, non-judgemental and genuine.
- The facilitator acknowledges the individual identity of each person.
- The facilitator is willing to use music, whether singing, voice work, percussion or guitar, etc. The approach relies on the simple rhythmic and melodic properties of music. Voice patterns similar to those used by caregivers during early interactions with infants are most helpful.

The facilitator takes responsibility for planning and organising resources and sessions. In this sense he or she also becomes the leader. As facilitator, and thus leader, we need to be acutely aware of our own powerful position and continually strive towards relinquishing control to learners. Confidence in practice, a good knowledge of Intensive Interaction (Nind and Hewett 1994) and the activities with which the group is concerned, is vital. A facilitator will display a real respect for the capacities of learners and encourage the creativity of all those in the group. We assume that all group members are 'speakers' and 'listeners'.

During the session the facilitator works primarily to acknowledge and extend communication. He or she develops a growing awareness and ability to pick up and reflect signals and actions from learners.

Central to the approach are the simple songs and activities, which are devised to encourage interaction on many levels. Each week during sessions the facilitator must ensure that some songs/activities stay the same in order to develop confidence through familiarity, but new or unexpected activities should always be offered to surprise, challenge and delight.

As the group gathers, the facilitator begins to sense the mood and concentrate on focusing all those present in a calm and confident way. A 'music time' gathering song is sung to signal the beginning and draw everyone together. Sung musical greetings follow as each child is sung to individually.

Let me now describe to the reader a typical Interactive Music session.

In the classroom chairs are ready in a circle. Support workers and a teacher gather with Molly, Ruth and John (not their real names) but we're still waiting for three more students to arrive. Let me introduce you to them. Molly smiles and giggles all the time; she has severe learning disabilities and a hearing impairment. She communicates through body language, gestures, vocalisation and eye contact. John is autistic; he is loud and aggressive and often displays self-injuring behaviours. He communicates through body language, by pulling on adults, banging on the table and through loud grunting vocalisations. He avoids eye contact. Ruth is very quiet; she avoids eye contact and displays a range of strategies in order to avoid participation (e.g. hitting). She communicates through body language, gesture, a little sign language and a vocabulary of about ten words.

The others arrive – now we begin. The sound of the guitar and gathering song signals the beginning. 'It's music time, it's music time, come and join me in a circle . . .' Each student is then sung to one at a time (the 'Hello' song reflects the season or theme). I observe and reflect students' feelings verbally or through the music. Today I'm worried about Ruth (she seems sad) and John is anxious after a disagreement at home.

In my mind I think we're going to the seaside (music and activities will reflect this). My huge fan introduces the theme; I waft it up and down, using rising intonation to exaggerate the words. It is irresistible; students feel the wind and follow the movements with their eyes. All of a sudden John jumps up out of his seat, flapping his hands and squealing. The focus of our attention moves towards him. I sing 'John, John, waving your hands, squealing, squealing and waving your hands' – the pace of the music is in time with his movements – and slowly, as he senses our interest, he begins to offer fleeting eye contact, first towards me and then his support worker. He rocks incessantly towards her – she mirrors his actions and vocalisation. I complement the interaction with a sung running commentary. An emotional connection is made, his anxiety acknowledged and this serves to change his mood. Eventually he is led back to his seat. 'Who wants the ocean drum?' I ask, and wait for a response. Molly reaches out – 'Oh, you want a turn,' I say, and off we go! Sounds of the sea made by the drum and the rhythmic quality of the song reinforce the theme and calm the group. The drum is passed around. Ruth pushes it away. 'Don't want a turn?' I say and it is passed on. Out come the instruments and novel sound-makers. Each group member, including staff, chooses – either by reaching, eye-pointing, vocalising or verbalising. Adults support but do *not* physically prompt. Students are enabled to explore the items as they wish. Ruth is joining in well. I reinforce her participation with a big smile and by mirroring her erratic rhythm on the guitar. In between each song 'burst' instruments are passed on in order to teach 'give and take', to offer a variety of experiences and to ensure everyone gets a turn of everything.

Time to collect in the instruments, 'In the bag,' I say. Students do this independently. John will not relinquish his instrument: 'That's okay, if you liked it so much,' I say. The blue silk cloth signals the peek-a-boo anticipation activity – it is fun, staff and students smile and laugh. The atmosphere changes, ''gain,' says Ruth – she gets a second turn . . . and so on. The session ends with a song. 'Music time is finished . . .' and finally, the goodbye song 'Until we meet again'.

Fisher (1990) discusses adult styles when teaching children to learn and think. He refers to adults as being either encouraging or inhibiting and lists 20 features of each. Encouraging adult: stresses independence, optimistic about outcomes, actively listens, is available, shares the risk; conversely inhibiting adult: authoritative, promotes dependence, predetermines response, limits time, inattentive, gives no feedback and so on. We do not want to take on an inhibiting role as it most certainly, in my experience, leads to negative outcomes.

Trouble-shooting

How much do I insist on participation?

First, what is participation? It means different things to different people. Essentially *you* provide the stimulating environment, *you* are open and ready for interaction, *you* continually 'read' learners' signals and *you* are willing to accept what a learner brings to the group on any particular day. This is a person-centred approach; our fixed agenda of games and activities must be flexible enough to celebrate anything and everything learners bring to a session, however little.

What do I do if a learner is not participating?

There are many reasons why a learner may choose not to participate. For example: lack of motivation, tiredness, illness, seeking attention through non-compliance, fear, sensory defensiveness or maybe they just don't want to or can't. There are no general rules: 'Never say never and never say always.' The important thing here is to listen actively to the person and follow their lead. Cajole and use what I call 'irritation strategies' (use an activity item to intrude sensitively, for example put it near the hand or other relevant body part and maybe tickle or tease) to get a reaction. Never force participation and avoid physical hand-over-hand prompts. Learners are not always required actively to take part. Where seemingly there is no participation, internally things will be happening.

How then do you interest and motivate the non-participator?

By using any spontaneous action/movement that learners possess (hands, eyes, head, feet, fingers, etc.). Start from their frame of reference – what they can already do. Activity items can be placed near to an active part of the body, allow time for responses and use irritation strategies to stimulate the learner. Take small steps, carefully observe and listen to the response. Follow their lead. Be patient. Depending on the situation, you may be able to play tickling games or engage the learners in interaction in some small way.

What do I do when a learner keeps leaving the group?

It depends. Learners are not forced to stay in the group; rather, they are gently encouraged to stay by directing them back to their chair as often as necessary. Learners may need time out of the circle, and this is fine. In an attempt to lure learners back into the circle, I endeavour to keep activity items within the circle and, if possible, keep the environment outside the circle unstimulating (hiding away or covering up favourite items). If a learner chooses to 'opt out' of the circle they are encouraged to relinquish activity items. Some learners may choose to stay outside all the time. Activity items, however, stay inside – you will know or get to know what motivates a particular learner; use these items to lure them back, whenever possible, even if only for short periods. To lure a learner back, call his or her name, hold up the favourite object and use positive encouraging body language, gesture and facial expression alongside your verbal encouragement (keep the language simple: 'John, do you want a turn? Come here' or just 'come').

What about learners who stand up a lot and always want to be in the middle?
Learners like this tend to love the 'limelight'. The difficulty is that they may steal it from others! The group as a whole will suffer if this one learner gets all the attention – in particular the quieter ones who don't push themselves forward. So, when such learners show by their action that they want to take centre stage, enable them to have their moment of glory in the middle and encourage interaction between and among others at this time – let them lead. After a 'fair' period, gently guide them back to their chair and, if necessary, be a bit insistent (assertive, not aggressive) that they have finished for now.

What about learners who put everything in their mouth?
Make sure objects are safe. Learners who mouth objects are likely to be at a sensory motor stage of development. By using this means of exploration they can learn about the properties and qualities of objects. Clean afterwards with anti-bacterial spray as required.

What do I do when learners throw everything or push things away?
How you deal with this depends on the object. Establish game routines using the learner's throwing action; perhaps tie a piece of ribbon to it so that it can be manipulated back and forth; or establish a 'give and take' throw and catch game, etc. Or hold on to the item, not in an insistent, intrusive way but so as to encourage focus of attention for a little longer before the push becomes insistent. Pushing away may mean 'No, thank you.' When this is the case we should accept this in order to build trust.

What do I do when learners continually drop objects?
I do not automatically pick up the object for them. In the natural infant–caregiver model, infants learn about object-permanence when they retrieve objects out of sight. Rather than pick up objects, use eye–hand pointing in order to make the learner aware of where the object is and to see if they will retrieve it for themselves. A learner may enjoy the give-and-take nature of you responding to their dropping, so this too may have value. Importantly, don't just pick up the dropped object for the sake of it; use the learner's deliberate action as a learning tool.

What about learners who have additional sensory deficit?
Observe and empathetically listen. Use material and activity items in such a way that makes access appropriate and comfortable via their strongest sense. Helpers may need to be more proactive here; for example, they may need to hold a drum near to an ear or offer the brightest colours (yellow is good) where visual impairment exists.

How do I motivate helpers who have difficulty with an activity?
Difficulties can arise for all kinds of reasons. Embarrassment may be one reason. This needs to be respected and the person encouraged and given the permission to opt out without feeling 'got at'. Learners, too, have the right to say no and this can build trust. Helpers should have a working knowledge of their role as communicator and role model. They may not understand what is expected of them, or may feel unable to 'come up with the goods'. You as facilitator must show by good example. Never expect anyone to do anything you yourself would not be willing to do. Talk to the person at a later date in a friendly and non-threatening way to discover where the blocks lie. It is likely that if they understand the process better, they will be more likely to participate appropriately.

What do I do if helpers constantly use negative reinforcement?
Ignore them! You can't change the habits of a lifetime overnight. People who seek to dominate and gain power over others, and in doing so think they can change behaviour, are likely to have been brought up with such notions from an early age. Instead, I accept (somewhat reluctantly) their position and attempt to teach by example. I try never to use negative reinforcement. If a helper acts negatively towards a learner I distance myself from their action and use every opportunity to reinforce positively that same learner. Equally I ignore a helper's bad behaviour and praise them for the good things they do. In human terms facilitators, helpers and learners are actually much the same.

All in all, I avoid confronting helpers; I might, however, gently say: 'Don't worry, I'll deal with it', or 'That's okay, let them do their own thing for a bit', or 'Shall we just see if he can manage by himself?' Phrases like this can prompt a negative 'reinforcer' to reconsider their position, but not always – this is a tough one. Gentle persistence and persuasion, rather than insistence, in my experience wins in the end.

In-service training in the use of interactive approaches can be a powerful way of reinforcing or getting the message across.

What do I do when helpers prompt too much?
This is a difficult behaviour to change. Helpers feel it is their job to prompt physically. If they do not step in and help, they may feel that they are not doing their job properly. Helpers may not know what to do instead. Standing back, actively listening and not 'doing' is much more difficult than 'doing'. Essentially, helpers need to learn the value of positive encouraging body language and exaggerated facial expression as a means of prompting. During group activities where everyone has an item, I always give one to helpers too. They act as role models and their musical contribution enhances the environment, but essentially, it also keeps their hands busy and prevents them from over-prompting.

Guidelines for helpers

Helpers' attitudes and their ability to pick up on and act upon learners' communication signals are key to successful outcomes. When helpers fail to recognise or choose to ignore communication attempts, however limited, the approach is compromised. Helpers have a key role – their mood (positive or negative) affects the outcome.

Helpers should:

- have access to and read this manual;
- adopt an interactive style of communication – one that responds to learners at their level, i.e. uses their 'language', as well as commenting upon and socially rewarding their interactive style;
- celebrate what the learner can do;
- pay attention to the facilitator and learner;
- provide feedback in order to inform future planning;
- be open to and respond to learners' intention to communicate;
- respond to communication signals at all times;
- model for learners' appropriate/alternative ways to explore and act;
- use encouraging and, if necessary, exaggerated facial and body expression to engage learners.

Helpers should not:

- deny learners their turn by intervening or prompting too early;
- use a hand-on-hand physical prompt in an attempt to show learners what to do. This may deny them their turn!
- force learners to do anything;
- distract learners at key points/pauses by adding extra verbal input or irrelevant conversation during learners' thinking or word-finding time;
- introduce topics that have nothing to do with the context of the session;
- talk while the learner is taking a turn;
- talk about learners as if they weren't there;
- become so involved in their own participation that they forget the needs of learners.

Guidelines for session planning

In order to motivate learners and sustain their interest, a session will need to include contrasting elements. Planning and preparation will ensure the balance is right. Using a variety of sensory materials alongside instruments and sound-makers provides opportunities for learners to receive input from various sensory experiences. The activities themselves are devised to intrigue and delight; the need, however, is to consider the possibilities that each activity holds for complementing and extending social interaction and communication. Remember, this is not a 'music' session in the sense that we want to teach musical skills!

Planning

Make a list of activities on a planning sheet. Consider arranging them so that one activity will focus on the group as a whole, and so that all members will be actively involved at one time. Follow this with an activity that focuses on each individual in turn. Announce, as often as is necessary, that everyone will get a turn and ensure that they always do. Provide a combination of routine and unpredictability, elements of surprise and delight and always some little or big item that is 'new' to the group. Remember, you have to be motivated to want to communicate, and learners will require something worthwhile (at their level) to communicate about.

The basic list (session plan) will act as security, offering a structure that avoids you having to think about what's coming next. However, the facilitator needs to be 'hyper-flexible' and to be prepared to adapt if things are going wrong. A favourite activity, maybe tambourine or hooter, can serve to refocus the group if and when attention drifts. Enabling learners to take the lead if they so desire will take confidence; but, I promise you, it will reap rewards and empower learners. In my experience, when enabled, learners' contributions can be amazing. Always be willing to alter ideas and hopes if you need to.

Duration

Sessions generally can run for up to an hour. The duration, however, depends very much on the group (size of group and ability level). Half an hour is sufficient for smaller groups.

Sessions will need to include:

- *Gathering* – a song or activity that signals the beginning.
- *Greeting* – a song that acknowledges each individual in turn.
- *Activities and games* that foster the ability to anticipate.
- *Burst-pause* activities in which the learner fills the pause.
- *A silly game* to encourage laughter.
- *A sung running commentary.*
- *Flexible interactive action or activity songs.*
- *Exploratory items.*
- *Opportunities* to develop awareness of cause and effect.
- *Farewell* – each person's contribution is mentioned and celebrated.
- *A song or activity* to signal the end.
- *A goodbye song.*

Preparation

Gather together instruments, sound-makers (home-made items often work best), materials and a range of other items such as feather dusters, a horn, ribbon sticks, etc. This is your basic tool kit.

Acquiring, making and preparing equipment takes time, thought and energy. You will need a special box, trolley or something in which to keep your activities and surprises. It is a good idea, but not always possible, for Interactive Music items to be used only during interactive sessions. This helps to keep them special, so learners will anticipate and look forward to them because they are not always readily available.

I suggest that you become a scavenger, visit second-hand shops, jumble sales, hardware shops and market stalls with intentional gusto! Everything (well, almost everything) may have an appealing element. If you write a song about it or create an activity around it you'll be surprised as to how, at this developmental level, its 'differentness' elicits various responses.

Be well prepared in order to give yourself and helpers confidence. Make sure the items you need are immediately to hand. Always have a few well-chosen extra items in case of unexpected eventualities. Ensure that all equipment is safe to be handled; I suggest as strong as a Tonka toy. For those not in my era, Tonka toys are the ones that elephants could stand on and not break. Keep your session plans in a file, as this will build into a wonderful resource for planning future sessions.

2 The Process

Interactive Music can reach learners on many levels and in many different contexts (home, school/college, care home, clinical/hospital setting, etc.). The multi-faceted nature of the approach and the fact that within each activity or song there is room for differentiation and improvisation according to learners' needs and developmental level makes it an incredibly versatile and useful approach

Interactive Music activities are presented within six areas of experience:

1. Enabling self-awareness
2. Valuing and extending communication skills
3. Nurturing playfulness
4. Creating stimulating atmospheres and environments
5. Encouraging exploration
6. Developing an openness to the joy and fulfilment of experience

Introduction to six areas of experience

The Interactive Music approach as a whole presents as multi-faceted, multi-dimensional and holistic. The focus primarily is on developing social communication; through the process, however, each facet of human nature is embraced. The six experiential areas: self-awareness, communication, exploration, joy and fulfilment of experience, playfulness, and creating atmospheres and environments merge to offer a positive framework for developing skills on many levels. As has already been mentioned, in order to communicate intentionally, learners must first want to communicate and then have something to communicate about (Coupe and Goldbart 1992). A multi-faceted approach provides the motivation learners require to look beyond themselves, to develop a greater understanding of their world and confidence in communicating.

In the early years of development, it seems evident that social and cognitive learning occur side by side. Social communication may well lie at the very core of intellectual and personal development (Vygotsky 1962, 1978), but learners, as Piaget suggested, need to construct actively their knowledge of the world by exploring objects and the world around them. 'Such sensory-motor learning is *structured* in the infant to form not only "internalised action" but ultimately *mental operations*' (Wood 1992:21). As learners reach for what they want, and learn to manipulate objects, so motor development also tends to show improvement.

During the process learners are not directly taught how to think, learn and communicate; rather, their ability to do so develops through the process of social interaction, by playing games and by learners' exploration of their physical world. Great care, as I have already stressed, needs to be taken when supporting students with hand-over-hand prompts. If prompting is used without due care and attention it simply denies learners the opportunity to achieve a desired outcome for themselves. Physical prompts should only be used as a last resort. Try gesture, exaggerated facial expression and positive reassuring body language first specifically to guide a learner towards the next stage of development. The steps here for 'our' learners are likely to be microscopically small. Consider every possible way in which a prompt can be delivered, in order to avoid damaging a learner's self-esteem.

The spiritual, too, is essentially contained within sessions. The SCAA report (1995) identifies eight dimensions of spirituality inherent in spiritual education:

1.   Beliefs
2.   The sense of awe, wonder and mystery
3.   Feelings of transcendence
4.   The search for meaning and purpose
5.   Self-knowledge
6.   Relationships
7.   Creativity
8.   Feelings and emotions

Within the framework of Interactive Music we do not dwell on the religious but rather embrace spirituality as something innate in all of us – that special something that makes the human species unique. Festivals and seasons are celebrated, moods are created, feelings acknowledged and relationships flourish. Priestley (1992:35) suggests, 'The greater purpose of education should be to give people a greater reliance on the validity of their own inward and private experiences.'

Interactive Music offers learners a cacophony of experiences, a range of opportunities and a humanistic person-centred approach that enables each of them to reach their full potential in human terms.

Enabling self-awareness

Self-awareness can be realised and expressed in a number of ways:

•   The person becomes aware of their identity and uniqueness.
•   The whole person feels nurtured – physical, emotional, spiritual.
•   The person knows that their communication behaviour has an effect.
•   The individual recognises and responds to their name.
•   The individual gains in confidence.
•   The individual understands more about their bodies.
•   The individual becomes aware of self in relation to others.
•   The individual becomes aware of ability.

Within an Interactive Music framework, learners can journey towards realising their full social potential. The all-important issue here is our attitude and behaviour towards them. An empathetic approach is essential. When the learner feels understood and valued, positive feelings towards the self are more likely to emerge. Further success, ability and confidence will surface if we enable and create opportunities for self-discovery. Learners will need to make decisions and choices, and to take responsibility for the consequences.

Our aim is always to build on success as opposed to failure in the sense of what they can't yet do. Persistent failure is damaging and tends to lead to low self-esteem. Worse, it can lead to learners giving up and not trying at all. High quality interactions are important and any dictatorial agenda needs to take a back seat. Ability may lie unrecognised and crushed if we fail to provide opportunities for active, person-centred learning.

Give every opportunity for learners to 'grow' and take control of their own learning. Hold high and not low expectations of what can be achieved; and finally, always remember to give them enough time and space to respond.

Valuing and extending communication skills

Aspects of communication skills are:

- Eye contact
- Attention
- Listening
- Gesture
- Anticipation
- Cause and effect
- Imitation
- Vocalisation
- Spoken language – meaningful or otherwise

The stages of normal development can serve as signposts for special needs educators who seek to develop fundamental communication and socialisation skills. Schaffer (1998) notes that a mother is seen to be responding to the infant in a way that gives intention to every aspect of the infant's behaviour. This notion should be mirrored within Interactive Music.

> The fact that you respond to the other person's signals of desire to initiate, maintain or terminate an interaction gives that person the negotiating powers to which he/she is entitled. (Nind and Hewett 1994:16)

Wells (1981) and Schaffer (1977a) both show the importance of an adult's response when a child attempts to convey meaning. Their findings confirm most effectively that he or she should assume the child has something to say, and respond by acknowledging the communicative significance. Wells discusses the likelihood that adults, who assume that children have capabilities, are actually enabling those capabilities to emerge. Learners whose gestured and behavioural attempts to communicate are not listened to or are misinterpreted by adults may well retreat into themselves or adopt inappropriate behaviour and suffer low self-esteem.

It is important to remember that we can easily use a learner's language. The learner, on the other hand, may never be able to use ours. Thus we have actively to listen to and learn each individual's particular language. Posture, body language, gesture, facial expression and vocal utterances are all relevant. In the communication process our reaction and the need to change our behaviour in order to let learners know that we are listening are of the utmost importance. We are trying to learn their language and we are ready for social interaction at their level.

Good learning, Vygotsky (1978) suggests, is that which is in advance of development – that which he called the 'zone of proximinal development'. This serves to acknowledge the actual developmental level of the learner and then to recognise the level of potential development. The 'gap' between the two is bridged with the assistance of a more able partner who supports what the learner is unable to achieve alone. When supporting, we need to be acutely aware that prompting can actually deny learners opportunities to learn. Sensitive prompting may be helpful, but over-prompting disregards the actual ability of a learner, and this, in turn, can destroy self-confidence and lead to a learner giving up. A much more helpful 'tool', I have found, is that of positive expectant body language where the helper/facilitator signals (without words) 'Go on – yes, you can do it.'

Fundamental communication

Subtle body movements
Eye movements
Mouth and tongue activity
Eye contact
Body 'stills'
Gasps
Changes of facial expression
Smiles
Changes of body posture
Turning away – usually means 'No, thank you'.
Gestures – leans forward, nods, reaches, hand and finger movements
Reach gestures
Pulling item towards themselves
Object/person eye contact
Vocalisation or any other sound, including laughter
Approximations to words, for example 'Yeah'
Pointing
Words and actions relevant to context

Eye contact

Eye contact is uniquely important. Unspoken messages are passed between communicators, and a kind of equality is established as each chooses whether or not to let the other person 'in'. Within the Interactive Music process eye contact is encouraged in a natural and spontaneous way. When eye contact enables a connection to be made, our response needs to be open and genuine so that learners discover that eye contact can engage people – our non-action may shut them out. A learner during Interactive Music can use eyes to engage others but also as a communication signal when making a choice (eye-pointing).

For some learners, those for example with profound and multiple learning difficulties, eye movements may be the only communication tool they have available to make choices. If they choose to avoid our stimulus, this should be respected, otherwise we deny them the only means they have of controlling their environment.

There is a notion that perhaps you can make or demand learners to 'look' at you. When this is the case, I believe that the value of such a 'look' is very small. Demanding offends and intrudes on that which is very personal. We should, I believe, avoid falling into the trap of saying 'Look at me', or, worse, using a physical prompt to turn someone's head in order to make them look. Alternatively, I suggest that facilitators are available and appealing to the learner. Schaffer (1977b) observed that during infant–parent interactions, parents manoeuvre themselves into positions that facilitate visual contact. Interactive Music seeks to emulate this by finding ways of encouraging eye contact in a creative, learner-centred way. Many activity items, for example, frame the face. Anticipation activities and expectant pauses also encourage eye contact in a natural, spontaneous and non-threatening way.

Attention

Attention can be very limited and this can lead to learners 'tuning out'. Within the Interactive Music framework we strive to maintain interest by creating a motivating environment, one that continually seeks to gain and maintain learners' attention by offering something worthwhile to communicate about at their level.

Many people with complex and multiple learning difficulties, however, do not automatically understand the 'rules' and 'norms' inherent during group work. The facilitator and helpers will need to learn to accept this and work within each individual's attention span, encouraging rather than insisting. 'Participation is an active, voluntary, constructive step on the part of the learner, compliance is doing what you are told to do' (Nind and Hewett 1994:76). This is a person-centred approach. We earnestly desire learners to participate but we do not insist on compliance.

You will need to be prepared to let learners enter or leave the circle if they are unable or unwilling to attend. A physical barrier created by helpers is often enough to encourage learners to stay within the confines of the group. If this fails, a decision made by a learner to leave is also seen as that person not wanting to take part. They should be encouraged therefore to relinquish items unless within the group. This is done in an attempt to lure them back into the circle where opportunities for social learning are being created. Do not force a learner to give you an item. Try persistent requesting, adopt an assertive stance and expectant body language. Keep language to a minimum and place emphasis on the use of key words such as 'Give'. If in the end they refuse to relinquish the item, step back into the circle and carry on. Present an activity that is likely to appeal to the 'non-giver' and perhaps they will then choose to rejoin the group. No one said it was easy; to a great extent your knowledge of a particular learner will guide your response and actions, but essentially the person-centred model should 'win'.

Gesture

A gesture is a physical signal, one where a part of the body is used as a signalling tool. This can range from tiny finger movements through to whole body gestures. It is vital that learners' physical communication signals are acknowledged and responded to by the facilitator and helpers. This can be difficult in a group situation, where more than one person may signal at the same time and where turn-taking is advocated. Nevertheless, it should be our goal to respond physically and verbally to signals and, where appropriate, to add intention to gestures. Schaffer (1998) notes that a mother is seen to be responding to the infant in a way that gives intention to every aspect of behaviour. When a learner reaches for an item you might say, 'Oh, you want a turn?'; the item is then given. If a child turns away, you might say: 'You don't want a turn'; the item is then moved away. In a group situation it is not always possible for learners to get what they want. They will have to learn to wait and to watch others with their favourite item. It is important here that we respond to gestures and don't ignore them, offering positive, friendly body language where the facilitator turns toward the learner, leans forward slightly, explains in a calm, non-threatening voice 'You have to wait' or 'Wait' (signing 'Wait' helps to reinforce visually what you are saying) or 'You've had your turn, give' or 'Give'. If they won't relinquish items, it's not the end of the world. Perhaps exchanging items will help. If necessary, let them continue until they are ready – which they may be when a more interesting item appears. Always positively reinforce willing giving.

We need constantly to observe learners and to be aware above all that sometimes gestures are very small and slow in coming – these, sadly, are the ones we so often miss.

Vocalisation

In order to maintain and maximise vocalisations, our response at all times should be interactive. This may mean imitating their sounds in order to set up a vocal conversation; listening to vocalisation in order to understand the meaning (is the sound distressed, happy, sad, etc.?) or responding by recognising vocalisations as a communication signal ('I want', 'Don't want', 'Go away', etc.). At a pre-verbal level, gestures and vocalisations often become consistent and ritualised. If others respond as if they were communicative signals, then communicative potential, I suggest, has every possibility of surfacing.

Vocal turn-taking is just like social 'chit-chat'. Enjoy!

Anticipation

Anticipation games such as 'Here I come – got you' offer facilitators a means for developing cognition. 'Practical intelligence takes the form of anticipating a state of affairs' (Wood 1992:20). If learners can imagine and anticipate a particular consequence, then it is likely that they are able to 'hold or represent what is sought in mind' (Wood 1992). Peek-a-boo games give pleasure and intensify social interactive episodes; again there is an element of expecting the unexpected and a means for developing cognition.

Cause and effect

When learners realise that their movements and language have an effect on their environment a connection is made between the cause (action/movement) and the effect (outcome). Learners, as they become aware that they can affect the environment, begin to learn that they can repeat an activity that was of particular interest – something they liked.

Cause and effect in social terms require a reaction from another person. Learners need to learn that their communication behaviour is affecting another's behaviour. When I do this, that happens. If the outcome makes them feel 'good', it is likely that they will want to repeat the experience.

Musical running commentary can be a useful tool in developing awareness because it complements and extends spontaneous actions/interactions. Here the facilitator makes up a simple song about whatever the learner is doing. For example, if the learner is tapping a foot the facilitator may sing: 'Tapping, tapping, John is tapping'. This song can then be extended to any spontaneous movement that the learner makes. It also gives them a time of freedom in the session where their movements are celebrated in order to give opportunities for them to take control over the interaction. By using this method and giving a consistent response to learners' spontaneous signals, an action can be given an intention and therefore a shared meaning.

Imitation

If a learner can imitate, learning may occur at a more sophisticated level. Importantly for us, when a learner does not imitate it is likely that he or she is unable to learn from just watching others. In particular, signing, though helpful as a visual cue, will be difficult to learn if the ability to imitate others is not established. When this is the case, physically prompting signs hand over hand is a waste of time!

Nurturing playfulness

Integral features of playfulness include:

- Having fun
- Spontaneity
- Letting go
- Play
- Experiences, activities and games
- Exploration and discovery
- Trial and error
- Imagination and creativity
- Sharing and reciprocity
- Friendship
- Physical contact
- What I can do
- What I want to do
- Action and reaction

Play within a non-judgemental, failure-free environment offers endless opportunities for exploration, discovery, observation, coordination and concept formation. It is a vital part of the growth and developmental process. Social play, where play and playfulness are shared with others, is essentially a communicative experience, one that encourages two-way processes to develop, such as social interaction, turn-taking and sharing. As positive feelings are generated, opportunities can be created to reinforce, practise and repeat what learners already know and can do. Playfulness develops a sense of together-ness between 'players' while maintaining the individuality of the person. Spontaneous encounters increase possibilities for mutual pleasure as well as self-satisfaction.

Playful activities within Interactive Music are personally and developmentally appropriate rather than age appropriate. The facilitator finds out about the learners' interests, what gains and holds their attention and what makes them laugh, etc. The facilitator makes use of this knowledge in order to develop activities and extend inter-active episodes. Spontaneous encounters seem to occur more freely when we use and celebrate the learners' ideas and capitalise on their playful behaviours in order to estab-lish play routines.

The importance of playfulness is highlighted by Nind and Hewett (1994) who recog-nise its huge value, both in human terms (because it causes pleasure) and as a teaching tool (because it proves motivating). Clearly, in the early years it has a huge impact on all areas of development by serving many different functions. These include: learning new skills through observation and exploration, concept formation, body awareness, physical activity, refining gross and fine motor skills, understanding emotion, develop-ing creativity, imagination, self-expression and encouraging peer interaction. Progress in social and cognitive terms is likely to depend on outcomes derived through play. Throughout the Interactive Music process elements of play and playfulness combine with social interaction routines; indeed, they are intrinsically linked.

Several activities (games with the hooter and lycra, for example) have been specifically designed to raise arousal levels and encourage playfulness. Games incorporating
elements of fun prove to be the most powerful in terms of engaging all group members
at the same time. Bringing fun to the learning environment goes some way to improv-
ing quality of life. Humour can make situations less threatening and this sometimes
helps to alter our perspective in ways that enable us to see more positive possibilities.
Positive attitudes towards learning seem to occur because laughter is viewed as something pleasant. It also offers a release from tension and encourages a more relaxed
approach when trying to understand others.

Strickland (1993) reports that physiological responses to laughter make you feel
good. She points to Berk's (1989) study, which describes how mirthful laughter appears
to reduce serum levels of cortisal, dopa epinephrine and growth hormones. The simple
act of laughter releases chemicals in the body that are natural painkillers – muscle
tension melts and stress levels drop. Laughter is viewed as something pleasant and thus
it has reinforcing properties. Everyone benefits!

Rough and tumble games such as 'Push and Pull', 'Tumbling', 'Tickling' and
'Jiggling' contain boisterous physical elements that may result in smiles or giggling.
These games may be useful for raising arousal levels, but during such games we must
be especially sensitive to learners' likes and dislikes. Be careful – don't invade body
space without permission. Listen to and read body language so that your intervention is
guided by them.

Anticipation games, Lycra games (see 'Lycra and the Flying Bird' in the Activities
section), sudden surprises, funny noises, wearing funny hats, etc. all engender a sense
of fun and help to create a positive learning environment.

Really let go of your inhibitions and enjoy episodes of shared fun. Mutual involvement provides wonderful opportunities for you and the learner really to get to know
each other. Fun, like music, offers a non-verbal means for communicating (smiles and
laughter). Words are not required.

Stages of play inherent in the Interactive Music approach

Social play

Social play refers to play that is not entirely solitary. Two or more people are involved.
Interaction is the key concept here and out of this come social play routines and reciprocal
game routines. Social play helps learners to learn about the two-way process of turn-
taking and sharing in human terms. Shared activity, especially when mutually pleasurable,
fosters a greater understanding of self and others.

Exploratory play

During Interactive Music sessions activity items provide learners with opportunities to learn about the properties and qualities of objects. Learners may not necessarily show the same curiosity when presented with such objects as their counterpart infants. In fact, in my experience, learners can often be very selective. 'Playing' with these items too can present as inappropriate if the developmental level of a particular learner fails to be taken into account. Sometimes, for reasons known only to each individual, play can become ritualised, repetitive and stereotypical. Objects then appear as comfort tools and consequently exploration tends to be limited. Here we may be able to share their kind of game by learning to play alongside. Exploratory play needs to be learner-led – their way and not ours. We help best when we encourage, admire and adopt their exploratory ideas.

Physical play

This involves developing awareness of our bodies and what they can do. Gross and fine motor skills can be refined and the movement patterns of the body explored. Whether sitting or moving, physical play can help with coordination and develop stamina. Some learners respond particularly well to elements of rough and tumble during play routines.

Constructive play

Purposeful use and manipulation of objects combine as motor and sensory skills integrate. Memory is involved and the ability to construct play objects, with the intention of achieving an outcome, is developed.

Creating stimulating atmospheres and environments

Factors to consider:

- Our senses
- Situational understanding
- Making sense of experiences
- Learning about change
- Making things special – seasonal or topic linked
- Using imagination
- Relaxation – being quiet and peaceful
- Surprising, noisy and invigorating
- Music and creative arts
- Colour

Create a therapeutic environment; a place that is safe, interesting and full of fun where learners can expand the depth and scope of experience through social interaction and creative sensory experiences.

At a sensory-motor stage of development, stimulation and information need to be provided at a fundamental level. There is also a need to 'tune in' to what interests and motivates each individual. Effective outcomes can be achieved when the interest, skill and aptitude of learners are recognised and considered during session planning.

Flo Longhorn (1988) saw the importance of sensory experiences for children who may be unable to sense, manipulate or respond to their environment in order to learn from it. Her idea of a sensory curriculum in the late 1980s was revolutionary and her ideas remain an integral part of special education programmes.

Music, scanned in the left side of the brain, thus linking it directly with our emotions, undoubtedly plays a central role in the Interactive Music process. I often recall the words of a song sung by Mary O'Hara over 20 years ago: 'Music speaks louder than words, it's the only thing that the whole world listens to.' These words encapsulate the universality of a phenomenon that generations of people have tried to explain. 'We cannot be free from it even if we so desired' notes Boethius (Storr 1992). Importantly, also, music is a non-verbal means of communication, one that can unite a group on many levels.

Novelty is one important aspect of stimulation that arouses curiosity and interest. Stimulation, however, needs to be presented in a way that not only gains attention but also recognises the fear and uncertainty that may be present within any particular group member. Sensitivity and selectivity according to learners' responses will help modulate their level of arousal while still encouraging participation.

Throughout the process we offer wide-ranging experiences. Each week some things stay the same in order to establish familiarity and create security, while on the other hand new and exciting surprises are also included. Getting the balance just right is a matter of practice and also depends on the mood of the group and what the learners want and can cope with.

With a wide range of interactive songs and activities a facilitator can both create moods and change the atmosphere. Sometimes a quiet, relaxing atmosphere is called for and at other times a noisy, boisterous and fun-filled atmosphere works best.

Rhythms inspired by nature and seasonal change can be embraced within sessions in order to awaken and refresh individual creativity. Seasonal creative experiences/activities help us all to connect with the wider world to which we all belong.

Points to remember when using sensory stimuli

Tactile – Students may dislike being touched or handled. They may be tactile-defensive, selective in what they touch or choose not to touch at all. A visual cue or touch signal offered prior to introducing tactile elements can help to prepare the learner. An empathetic understanding for the person on the receiving end is essential.

Visual – What you see (particularly colours) triggers a range of emotions including exhilaration, fear, calmness and joy. Visually presented stimuli can help to reinforce the theme of an activity and help to gain and maintain attention. Each activity item can also act as an object of reference by visually signalling what is coming next. Look out for and take account of any visual impairment and adjust what is being offered accordingly.

Auditory – The human ear is the first human sense organ developed in the womb. Vocal expression, sounds and music offer a means for developing greater understanding of the environment, and, when vocalising, a better understanding of oneself. Some learners may be sound-sensitive and others may have a hearing impairment of one kind or another. Take care; sound can be painful. The sound of silence can be a powerful tool when attempting to build tension, and silence, too, can create space for learners to fill.

Taste – This is closely linked with the development of smell. It is possible to increase the learner's experience of an activity through taste and textures, but generally this sensory channel is not targeted during Interactive Music. Learners who mouth objects in order to get a sense of what they are may, however, experience sensations via taste.

Smell – Sense of smell varies greatly from person to person. Look for likes and dislikes. Smell can help learners to recognise and discriminate between particular activities and different people. Linked with memory, it can act as an anticipatory tool. Generally, smells are not considered during planning; rather, they tend to occur naturally!

Encouraging exploration

Aspects of exploration include:

- Looking and listening
- Touching and feeling
- Tasting and smelling
- Similarities and differences
- Action–reaction
- Doing
- Discovery and investigation
- Visual and tactile awareness
- Concept formation

At a sensory-motor stage of development, stimulation and information need to be provided at a fundamental level. Information about properties and functions of objects (object concept) dominates early learning (Schaffer 1998). Learners need to explore objects before they develop concepts of objects. We must acknowledge the developmental level of the learner and then enable exploration at that level. Learners develop thoughts and ideas about objects through their own exploratory ideas – theirs and not ours or what we would like them to be. We need also to be aware that for some learners, stimulation from objects may be preferred to human interaction. During the exploration process physical prompting should be non-existent or absolutely minimal – *enabling rather than controlling*. Let them make their own discoveries and learn from their own mistakes. Positive, expectant body language and verbal praise are often enough to encourage extended exploration.

Visual elements used within sessions increase attentiveness. That which is novel, bright and colourful holds the possibility of arousing interest and curiosity. When a large Chinese fan, for example, is wafted up and down, learners feel the wind, and invariably, because of its colour and beauty, are drawn towards following its movements. Visual elements offer a clue as to what is going on and activity items signal what is coming next.

The relevance of tactile sensory input at this developmental level is acknowledged – equipment works at the level of learners. When observing learners' exploration, three questions can be asked: Have learners developed a concept of objects? (Piaget 1952) What is the learner's own perceptual awareness of objects? How can the social experiences we create facilitate an understanding of objects? A learner will need to perceive that an object is the same object wherever and however it is presented. Object permanence occurs much later when learners realise that an object exists even when it can no longer be seen or acted upon. The identity of the object, that is whether or not it can be recognised in varying contexts, also proves difficult for some of our learners.

The mother's role is seen to be one of establishing topic sharing and object–person play. She draws attention to objects by pointing and naming. It is not until the end of the first year that 'another person's gaze direction becomes meaningful' (Schaffer 1998). The mother, as facilitator, follows the child's lead by attending to and extending exploratory play ideas. She names objects and offers a commentary to reinforce ideas and extend the infant's knowledge of the world.

When learners use instruments or activity items, allow them to make their own discoveries. If they are developmentally young, it is very likely that they will want to explore rather than 'play' the instrument – enable and encourage this because it is a vital part of the learning process. Remember, also, that learners when 'mouthing' objects may actually be learning about the properties of objects in a stimulus-driven way.

Although the main thrust of Interactive Music is to develop communication, the approach, being multi-faceted, also aids learning in all areas of development. Some of the cognitive and motor developmental aims are to:

- develop an interest in objects;
- fix a gaze on an object;
- follow moving objects (track);
- develop hand–eye coordination;
- locate and track sounds;
- discriminate and make choices;
- develop awareness of cause and effect;
- improve gross-motor skills;
- touch and develop an ability to distinguish by feeling;
- develop fine-motor finger control;
- develop muscular control;
- improve visual-motor coordination;
- develop manipulation skills;
- explore shapes, texture and weight in order to develop object concept;
- learn about sequencing;
- learn about object–person;
- anticipate;
- problem-solve;
- learn object permanence.

Developing an openness to the joy and fulfilment of experience

Joy and fulfilment can be realised and experienced by:

- being positive;
- developing an awareness of feelings and emotions;
- celebrating;
- delighting in one another;
- mutual pleasure;
- excitement;
- freedom;
- spiritual awareness;
- peace.

Some years ago, when I started to develop Interactive Music, I wrote about the light within people – their essence, something which is unexplainable. It is this notion that remains at the very centre of my personal philosophy and subsequently at the centre of this approach. Human beings hold physical, mental and spiritual properties. They are each special and unique. I believe that a holistic approach, feeding each of the human facets, needs to be embraced if a 'true' and honest human connection is to be made. Let us seek to embrace and connect with the whole person.

> Though the human body is born complete in one moment, the human heart is never completely born. It is being birthed in every experience of your life. (O'Donohue 1999:26)

Our 'inner story' affects our life – it makes us who we are. Spirituality is part of our internal map; whether or not we choose to engage with God is a personal matter. I agree with Stone (1995) who points out that 'Spiritual experience, whether or not derived from a religious tradition, is a key factor in the way in which a person sees the whole of life.' I am passionate about my own spirituality, and therefore in this chapter I indulge myself a little and ask: are those with special needs being offered appropriate opportunities to become aware of their spirituality? Knowing God should be a matter of free choice. I speak of God in the wider sense of the word: God as creator, sustainer, provider, healer; God of beauty and nature; God as Father or Mother figure, etc. People, including those with profound and severe learning difficulties, should be given the opportunity to decide for themselves. Faith and awareness of one's own spirituality, in my experience, brings inner peace, joy and contentment.

Assemblies are full of certificates and worldly themes and, more often than not, spirituality tends to take a back seat. In order for collective worship to underpin spiritual growth, a special time, one that is uniquely different from the rest of the day, should be set aside. This space should enable interaction, reflection, stillness and peace as well as joyous celebration. It is in these very spaces that learners can be given the opportunity to 'travel' inwards, a chance to reflect on their relationship with others, with God and with the world around them. A space such as this should offer learners freedom to respond in ways appropriate to each individual within their own belief system. Here you might learn about your inner story and find peace and a sense of calm in a world that all too often reflects the outer story.

During Interactive Music sessions, there is not an overt intention to bring the spiritual into the proceedings. It arrives naturally, in moments of joy and awakening, as relationships blossom, when the sun shines and all is well with the world; at sad times when sorrow is shared, when peace reigns; and especially so when human hearts meet.

In the field of special needs, Intensive Interaction, pioneered by Nind and Hewett (1994), goes some considerable way towards recognising, accepting and acknowledging humans as uniquely special. That invisible something occurring when partners 'tune' in to each other is captured without that being the intention. They stress, as do I, that we need unequivocally to respect and honour all those with whom we work. This may be idealistic and at times difficult to achieve, but as an aim it ought surely to be at the top of all our agendas.

I am thrilled when a connection is made, that moment when two people are open and eager to enter each other's inner world in a way that is honourable, non-judgemental and respectful of human dignity. When this 'true' connection is established, spirits meet and a kind of inner freedom pervades. Here an emotional experience occurs that seems to go beyond body and mind. 'Two people who are really awakened inhabit the one circle of belonging' (O'Donohue 1999). Friendship can be fostered and trust confirmed.

Without a doubt, our understanding of this 'tuning in' process offers learners a pathway to fulfilment in human interactive terms. If the process of 'tuning in' is merely an educational exercise, however, or a half-hearted gesture, the 'magic' will not work – a meaningful connection undoubtedly will not be made. This fundamental human experience has to be established by two willing people, and the learner's inclination to enter this abyss may be as fragile as ours.

And finally . . .

Throughout this manual I have drawn parallels between early infant development and the development of our 'special' learners. While there are differences, much can be learned. The behaviour of the caregiver, for example, which often revolves around the infant's agenda, offers, I believe, an excellent model. As educators we must find new ways to *adjust our behaviour* in order to facilitate learners' communication development. At an early developmental level, learners become socially empowered when facilitators and helpers make what they say and do contingent upon the learner's behaviour. Dictatorial agendas need to take a back seat.

Without a deep respect and genuine belief in the ability of those we seek to reach, our role as educators, I suggest, may become less than satisfactory. Our responsibility must surely go beyond the realms of providing a broad and balanced curriculum; rather, it should consider individual need and quality of life. Learners' needs in so many ways are very similar to our own. They don't like failure, they feel hurt when people continually scold them, give up trying when their efforts are not recognised, lack confidence when people insinuate they can't do something and feel ugly because of the way people look at them and treat them. Equally, they, too, desire to be liked, to feel valued, to feel that their contribution (however small) is worthy of comment and praise, to feel proud, to know that their ideas are important and that they are good to be with.

Eyes Look at Me

They stare and I see anger in that stare
They smile and I see joy in that smile
They gaze and I see openness in that gaze
They look and I see questioning in that look
They sneer and I see resentfulness in that sneer
They squint and I see hurt in that squint
They glance and I see maybe in that glance
They twinkle and I see playfulness in that twinkle
They sparkle and I see fun in that sparkle
They draw me in and I feel accepted

3   The Activities

The songs and activities presented in this chapter have been devised to develop funda-mental communication and social skills. If the person-centred philosophy is abandoned in favour of using these songs during prescriptive music sessions, then the essence of Interactive Music is lost. *The interactive 'bit' must be at the heart of each activity and game routine.*

An introduction to using the activities

All activities have been created to enable learners' actions to affect the outcome. It is this that enables learners to obtain a sense of their own importance and develop a growing awareness of their own ability to be effective communicators within a social setting. Activities should be presented at a pace that learners can understand; this makes it different from educational music time where, most likely, songs are sung as they are written. Songs are repeated as often as necessary to accompany each person's turn. Sung/musical improvisation reflecting learners' actions works very well.

During sessions, if a spontaneous interactive moment occurs, abandon the activity and go with the flow of the interaction. If you are not used to doing this, it does indeed take great courage and confidence; as educators we tend to cling to the security of a structure. Give it your best shot; once freed from the 'slavery' of rigidity, educational and personal rewards can be enormous.

While the activities are being presented, the facilitator and helpers alike play a key role by looking for, being open to and acknowledging attempts to interact and 'connect' in human terms. The facilitator, in particular, must demonstrate an openness to be flexible within each song or game routine, an earnest desire to listen actively (not just with ears and eyes but with the heart also) and a willingness to shelve the notion of working towards pre-determined objectives. Rather, celebrate that which each particu-lar learner, on that particular day, brings to the session. This will help learners to feel valued, empowered and understood.

I mention objectives only briefly. While they can be burdensome if allowed to over-ride the process, they are in fact an important part of the structure. Objectives, when empathetically set, can provide a hidden agenda that helps the facilitator to work towards developing social communication. During Interactive Music sessions, objec-tives can be borne in mind but the process should remain entirely flexible in order to meet the learner where he or she is. 'The teaching style is interpretive rather than directive and the power base of the learning is shared between the teacher and the learner during interaction sequences' (Nind and Hewett 1994:14).

Objective setting can, I believe, be inappropriate but we should be looking for ways of extending that which learners can already do. Objectives therefore need to be realistically set. Those writing them should be well informed about the nature of social and cognitive development, and in particular have a sound knowledge base as to how communication develops in infancy. Assessment should be ongoing and outcomes should be recorded, in order to inform future evaluation and session planning. This is common sense!

Contingent teaching, where a facilitator/helper begins with whatever the learner can do and then highlights that which needs to be taken account of in order to support learning at an appropriate level, also helps. Possibilities for development are built in by 'scaffolding' (Wood *et al.* 1976 in Wood 1992) – timely intervention that supports the learner to achieve the next step.

Providing developmentally appropriate environments infused with responsive interactive human support enables learners to succeed. Create a failure-free zone where 'the emphasis is on the exploring, the doing and the discovery' (Nind and Hewett 1994). This offers learners the best chance of fulfilment and development.

Don't 'waste' these songs and interactive activities in search of musical development; rather, use them to your heart's content to develop people's ability to share in life's wonderful social tapestry.

Once you have taken on board this interactive way of working and have an appreciation of how the activities work, consider using your own creativity to develop your own activities. Many adults with whom I have worked have said things like 'I don't know if I can do this' or 'I'm not musical and I can't even sing'; they now write their own songs and create their own activities.

The activities in this book, in many ways, are just a starter. Do not use them to the exclusion of other good 'stuff'. Add your own ideas, songs and games, but always insist on the interactive aspect remaining at the centre of what you do. It is this that makes the approach different – *flexibility* within a structured framework; learners share, control, direct and guide the process, and the facilitator and helpers delight in their ideas.

Likewise, do not let Interactive Music become boring by using the same old songs over and over again. Ring the changes; keep selected favoured ones in your repertoire but always ensure you offer new, novel and intriguing activities. The process develops and grows and so stays alive.

General guidelines – a reminder

- Learners are not always required to take an active part. Music relates directly to the learner's inner world; where there seems to be no participation, internally things will be happening. If a learner chooses to opt out, consider also that this may be for a very good reason.
- Anxiety caused by lack of understanding, either social or environmental, may also trigger a 'switch off'. New activities may cause anxiety and some activities may not be sufficiently motivating to cause interest and participation.

- Intervention in the form of physical prompting is not usually necessary. Learners need to access objects (instruments, sound-makers, etc.) at a level that is developmentally appropriate. Exploration should generate from the learner – their ideas and not ours or what we would like them to be. Learners learn from their own discoveries and from their own mistakes. Use positive encouraging, reassuring body language and exaggerated facial expression to encourage participation.
- Do not assume that where a learner has aggressive tendencies or challenging behaviour that he or she will be disruptive or violent with activity items. Give equal opportunities for them to explore while closely supervising. Try not to anticipate the worst, and especially don't let them see that you think they might act inappropriately. If you say for example 'Don't throw it or you won't get a turn' you may actually be feeding them with the idea of throwing. Rather, build trust by holding a high expectation that they will indeed manage to achieve.
- Avoid confrontation.
- Take care not to judge by making verbal comments about what learners cannot do.
- Avoid negative reinforcement. Rather, use positive reinforcement at every opportunity – not just verbally but via facial expression and body language also.
- If learners have a limited attention span or find it difficult to sit for long periods of time, enable them to have time outside the circle. If possible, keep activity items within the circle. If the activities are motivating enough, the learner will want to take part.
- Support, but don't do it for them. Let them know that their actions and not yours are determining the outcome.

The Ten Commandments of quality interaction

1. Actively listen with your heart as well as your ears.
2. Provide listener feedback (positive body language and facial expression) to ensure the learner knows you are listening.
3. Make others feel valued.
4. Be genuine.
5. Learn your partner's 'language' and consider adopting their style during interaction.
6. Consider proximity.
7. Observe the outer 'story' but reflect upon and consider the inner 'story'.
8. 'Tune in' at an emotional level.
9. Respect yourself and others.
10. Smile, play, relax and enjoy each other's company.

Key to songs and activities

❍ Enabling self-awareness
⁂ Valuing and extending communication skills
◇ Nurturing playfulness
❒ Creating stimulating atmospheres and environments
⊙ Encouraging exploration
☺ Developing an openness to the joy and fulfilment of experience

Altogether Quietly

Items required

Just people.

Activity

This is a calm repetitive relaxation song. Humming the tune can further support this activity. During relaxation activities read and follow learners' signals and be guided by their response. Helpers can sway gently from side to side and hold learners' hands, stroke back, arms or hands. Change the words of the song to support any spontaneous actions made by learners or helpers.

Consider

A large piece of 'floaty' material (sari, for example) could aesthetically support this quiet time. Here two helpers hold either end as the sari is wafted up and down.

Key: ○ ✳ ❐ ☺

Altogether Quietly

Bubbles

Item required
Bubble-blowing equipment – a bubble gun is perfect.

Activity
A helper goes into the inner circle and becomes the bubble blower. Bubbles are blown all around the circle and sometimes towards individuals. This is a pleasant, satisfying activity. Everyone loves bubbles.

Consider
Instead of singing 'Bubble, bubble, bubble, bubble [bubble]' sing 'Bubble, bubble, bubble, bubble [name]' in order to personalise the experience.

Key: ◇   ❑   ☺

Bubbles

Disco Tambourine

Item required
A tambourine – the cause and effect battery-operated flashing type is perfect, but any one would do.

Activity
Turn-taking activity. Ask individuals if they want a turn. Encourage reach gesture, vocalisation or language according to level of ability. Subsequently the tambourine can be passed on, thus encouraging give and take; or following an instruction, the tambourine can be given to a particular group member.

Consider
If learners have difficulty with the notion of 'Give', ask them to hand the tambourine to a helper rather than another learner. The helper can use verbal or gestured prompts in order to encourage a positive outcome.

Key: ✳ ◇ ◻ ◉

Disco Tambourine

Dressing-up Day

Items required

Dressing-up items – wigs, hats, masks, sunglasses, etc. and also a mirror.

Activity

Dressing-up items are placed on the floor in the centre of the circle. Supported by the song, each group member in turn chooses from what's on offer, and if they so wish (they may prefer just to explore the item or to see you wearing it), proceed to put it on. Help and support may be required – mirrors can be used to make this activity more fun while also providing opportunities to develop self-awareness.

Consider

Ensure learners are enabled to make choices about how they participate. Don't force anyone into wearing anything. Being given the freedom to choose is what is important here. Helpers wearing hats can draw attention to the face, and this, in turn, creates opportunities for interaction.

Not necessarily relevant to this activity but worth mentioning: beware of face paints – before you even think of putting them on learners' faces let someone put them on your face, with your eyes closed, and see how it feels! Personally I hate it!

Key: ○ ✳ ◇ ❑ ☉ ☺

Dressing-up Day

Feeling Hands

Items required
Just people.

Activity
This is an interactive 'talking hands' activity where both partners can communicate through touch. Touching strategies can range from stroking to tapping. Learners' movements can be very slight; wait, observe and actively listen to ensure the movement ideas are not always yours. Humming the tune can further support this activity.

Consider
Change the words of the song to signal change of activity, for example: 'Rocking together so nicely' or 'Feeling feet so nicely' or 'Rubbing your back so nicely' and so on.

Key: ○ ❈ ▢ ☺

Goodbye Song

A goodbye song signals the end of a session. A short plenary should precede this to enable each learner's participation to be commented upon and celebrated.

Gloves for Our Fingers

Item required
A bag of gloves – different colours and textures.

Activity
All helpers choose and then put on a pair of gloves. This is an interactive activity. Each helper offers a learner their gloved hands. The interaction that follows is led by what the learners do and how they interact. They may like to feel, clap your hands together, play peek-a-boo, etc. At the end of each song-burst, helpers move on to interact with another learner. All learners are able to interact with all the helpers.

Consider
Acknowledge likes and dislikes of learners. Although this is a learner-led activity, opportunities for sharing control can be incorporated if appropriate.

Key: ◖ ✳ ◇ ⬛ ⊙ ☺

Gloves for Our Fingers

Got You

Item required
A 'Got you' hat (special to this activity) or any visual activity item that could act as a point of 'Got you' reference.

Activity
Supported by the song, a helper moves around the inner circle in a teasing 'Coming to get you' kind of way. The helper's name is used. The helper will decide who is ready to be got by acknowledging the individual's expectant behaviour. On 'Are you ready?' (pause and wait for anticipatory communication signal) the helper gives the learner a rough and tumble, jiggling a reward on 'Got you'.

Consider
Rough and tumble play, tickling, etc. should always be delivered with sensitivity and consideration as to the likes and dislikes of learners.

Key: ◗ ✳ ◇ ☺

Group Instrumentals

Items required

Instruments and sound-makers. I often use a variety because learners may prefer, for example, to explore and shake bells (Christmas tree decorations) rather than traditional instrumental varieties. I have a number of instruments in each category. Tambourines, for example, can be sophisticated quality instruments or those bought in toy or second-hand shops.

Activity

A group instrumental activity will invariably be part of your weekly session. All group members have an instrument. Learners are free to explore them as they wish, while helpers, if not supporting, can play suitable rhythms to enhance the musical environment. Following a song-burst instruments are passed on to the next person, partly to encourage 'give and take' but also to ensure that everyone has an opportunity to use each instrument. This is important as it builds trust and helps learners to be patient in waiting for a favoured item.

Depending on ability, stop-and-go cues can be used as well as changing dynamics: quiet, loud, fast and slow, etc. Everyone participates independently at their own level.

Instrumental interludes can provide opportunities to introduce songs and chants relevant to themes or the time of year. In order to make them interactive, however, it is often necessary to change or modify the words. For example, during 'Jingle Bells', instead of singing 'dashing through the snow' sing: 'John plays the bells, John plays the bells, John plays the bells, oh, John play the bells'. In this way a variety of songs can be incorporated into sessions throughout the year. Capitalise on opportunities for communication and always remain flexible and responsive to learners' ideas. Sometimes enable learners to choose between instruments. A particular learner may be chosen to give instruments out and another to collect them in. Always encourage the use of language relevant to the context. Ask them to name instruments, theirs or others. See if they can use verbs and adjectives to describe them and so on.

Key: ✳ ◇ ❑ ⊙

Here Comes the Band

Items required

Enough instruments and sound-makers (anything that makes a sound) for all group members.

Activity

Give each learner an instrument, expect a reach gesture or signal that lets you know they want an instrument or allow them to choose an instrument, either from a bag or by holding out two for them to choose from.

Sing the song as many times as you need to in order to support exploration and playing. During a pause say 'Pass it on'; learners then pass on their instrument to the person sitting next to them. In this way they can practise 'give and take'. Helpers should encourage learners to do this for themselves. Ensure everyone gets a turn at everything.

Consider

During the band song, instead of singing 'Here comes the band la la', etc. sing 'Here comes the band, here comes the band, it's a Christmas [or any other theme] band today'. For more able participants use 'Stop' and 'Go' signals. Maybe learners can choose when to say 'Stop' and 'Go'. Instructions can also be given to play quietly or loudly, etc.

Key: ☽ ✳ ◇ ❑ ⊙

Here Comes the Band

Hello, Everyone

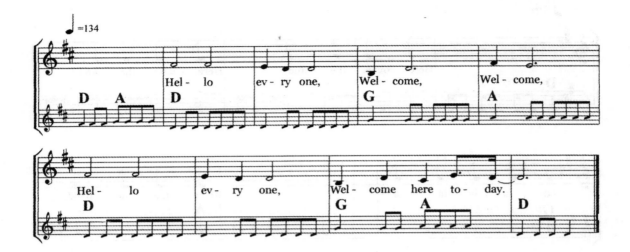

During each repetition of the song use each individual's name. Leave space for each person to respond according to his or her ability. Where there is no spoken language a two-way, non-verbal exchange may occur.

Hooter

Item required

A horn. If you can acquire one, the old-fashioned large car horns are wonderful. If not, a bicycle horn may do.

Activity

The facilitator moves around the inner circle. A verbal warning is issued as to the loudness of the sound and then a 'hoot' is delivered into the air. What happens next depends on the ability of the learners.

1. Facilitator says 'Ready steady' and during an expectant pause awaits a signal 'Go'; the hoot reward is delivered onto a person's body as soon as they signal or show signs of anticipation.
2. Facilitator says 'Ready steady'. . . during the pause the learner pulls the 'hooter' towards themselves. Hoot!
3. Facilitator says 'Ready steady, where', expectant pause awaiting a physical or verbal signal as to where the learner would like to be 'hooted' on.
4. Find rhyming words to body parts.
5. To encourage peer interaction a learner leads the activity. Sensitive physical and verbal prompting may be helpful in the early learning stages. We need to be prepared to accept approximations but learners may need to be encouraged to wait and listen to the other person to discover where the hoot goes.
6. The facilitator/helpers ask to be 'hooted' on by using a sequence of instructions. For example, 'Hoot on my foot first and then on my tummy' and so on.

Consider

According to ability, encourage language responses during the pause such as 'Go'. 'Yes' or 'No' responses can be sought by asking them if they want a turn.

If an inappropriate part of the body is chosen, say: 'No, I'm sorry, we don't do that one'.

Key: ◯ ✳ ◇ ❒ ☺

Jingle Gloves

Item required

One pair of shiny evening gloves to which you attach small (safe) Indian bells to the top of each finger.

Activity

With the musical support of the song, a helper wears the gloves and creatively moves around the inner circle; all the time jingling fingers towards group members. On a sung cue 'Jingle, jingle, jingle', move towards a particular person and proceed to jingle on a particular body part. Here the facilitator follows the lead of the helper who in turn has been guided by the learner as he or she sings the name of the body part that is being jingled upon.

Consider

Sensitivity is essential. Jingling should be gentle and non-threatening. Avoid direct jingling towards the face as this can be alarming for unsuspecting learners. Read body language to inform you as to where they might like to be jingled on.

Key: ○ ✳ ◇ ☺

Jingle Gloves

Lycra and the Flying Bird

Items required
Lycra – 2½–3 m is sufficient and an Emu-type bird or similar.

Activity
This is a group activity. Learners hold on to the edge of the cloth if they themselves choose to. Helpers and facilitator hold on to the cloth and facilitate its movement up and down. The bird is thrown into the middle, with helpers and facilitator saying 'On the cloth'; it is then tossed up and down into the air. If the bird lands on someone they can explore it for a while. Alternatively, the facilitator can manipulate the situation so as to grab the bird and place it somewhere on his or her body. In this way students can be encouraged to use prepositions: 'Under your arm' or 'On your head, for example. This is a wonderful fun activity – I dare you not to enjoy it!

Consider
All manner of objects can be placed on Lycra to cause different effects and elicit different responses. Giggle-balls rolled on top of the cloth can be fun, and large sparkly balls attract attention. Learners' favourite items ('twiddlers' or sparkly paper, for example) can be used.

Key: ◯   ✳   ◇   ❑   ⊙   ☺

Music Time

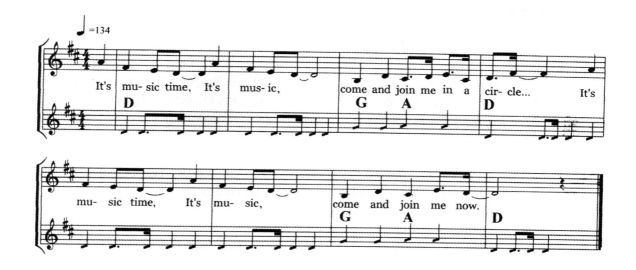

I use this gathering song at the beginning of every session.

Mirror Song

Item required
A mirror – a safe one, ideally plastic.

Activity
Each learner, in turn, will have a chance to look into and explore the mirror. The song, which includes the use of each individual's name, supports the activity. Change the words of the song to offer a commentary on what each individual does.

Consider
Mirror work can be lots of fun, so this is an activity for all to enjoy. Remember, also, that learners may prefer to play with, rather than look in, the mirror.

Sharing a mirror (learner/helper) while the facilitator sings about what happens (sung running commentary) extends learners' exploration and interactions.

Stickers placed on a face (little white paper eyelets work well) can draw attention to the face. If sticking them on a learner's face, make sure it's okay with the learner.

Key: ◗ ✳ ◇ ⊙ ☺

Mirror Song

Ocean Drum

Item required
An ocean drum.

Activity
This activity could start with the facilitator wandering around the circle holding the drum over the heads of group members. This is done to offer a unique sound experience but also to encourage learners to look upwards and to track the drum as it moves away. The song then supports individual exploration and turn-taking at all levels.

Consider
The ocean surf sounds can be hypnotic so this activity offers a means of creating a calm and focused atmosphere. I sometimes use this song as a 'Hello' song: 'John says hello with the ocean drum', etc. or as a song to say goodbye.

Key: ◖   ✲   ◇   ⬜   ◉   ☺

Ocean Drum

Rainbow Ring

Item required
A home-made Rainbow Ring. I made mine by threading lots of different coloured lids (plastic milk-bottle type) on to a strong piece of twine. It measures approximately 65 cm but when drawn around into a circle it is about 30 cm in length. I made the holes in the plastic bottle tops with a hot poker.

Activity
Ask individuals if they want a turn. Encourage eye-pointing, a reach gesture, vocalisation. If possible, encourage language or signed response.

The song supports the learners' 'free' exploration. Encourage and develop any language learners may possess and celebrate their ideas and actions.

Consider
Learners can take their turn in a variety of ways. Some may choose to put it over their head and just wear it. The accompanying song enables sung running commentary so that learners' actions can be acknowledged and their participation reinforced. For example, 'Feel the colours', 'Listen to the colours', 'Shake the colours', etc. Sing about whatever they do by changing the first word of each line within the song.

Key: ◔   ✳   ☐   ⊙

Rainbow Ring

Rainmaker

Item required

A rainmaker (any variety).

Activity

This song supports the individual's exploration of the rainmaker. During the activity turn-taking can occur in a variety of ways. The rainmaker can be passed on to the next person or given to another group member on instruction from the facilitator.

Consider

Learners may be unable to manipulate accurately or turn the rainmaker around. This may not be necessary as rainmakers make sounds in other ways. It may, on the other hand, be necessary to prompt or actually turn the rainmaker for the learner. Take care not to impose your own exploratory ideas upon learners. Let them discover how to do it for themselves. It may be that they just want to hold it and roll it on their leg, for example.

If the rainmaker is a large one, ensure that when turned, it doesn't hit the adjacent person!

Key: ◯ ✳ ◇ ❑ ⊙ ☺

Rainmaker

Scarecrow

Items required
A bag, a long jacket with patches sewn on, a flippy-floppy scarecrow hat, an old scarf and a pair of unusual gloves.

Activity
A helper supported by the song gradually dresses up during the song. A helper will need to adopt an interactive style and involve learners throughout by moving towards them in order to make the scarecrow items explicit. Each item in turn comes out of the bag. Follow a specific order when dressing – the song will support this. A flippy-floppy hat . . . a jacket full of patches . . . a lovely orange wig . . . a scarf that's full of holes, some gloves that look like hands. When all verses and choruses in between are sung, your helper will have become the scarecrow. Sing 'Oh we have made a scarecrow ooh argh', etc.

The Dingle Dangle Scarecrow song (an adapted version) is now used as an anticipation activity. Supported by the first few lines of 'I'm a Dingle Dangle Scarecrow' go to each learner in turn. Sing 'I can touch/shake your hand like this and . . . [rising intonation] tickle your . . . [pause for response in case they want to be tickled in a particular place – if not you choose] like that'.

Consider
A 'Gimme five' activity can be incorporated instead of a handshake if this is more appropriate. To encourage peer interaction enable learners to take a lead role. They dress up as the scarecrow and subsequently direct the physical interaction. Physical and verbal prompting may be necessary at first as learners practise the sequence.

Key: ◯   ✳   ◇   ◻   ☺

Scarecrow

Play the Drum

Item required

Any drum will do, but not too big because it will need to be passed on.

Activity

During this activity each learner takes a turn to explore or play the drum. In between each turn, when passing on, learners use whatever communication skills they possess. As facilitator we encourage 'give and take', or exchange; instructing them to give it to a particular named person or asking them to choose who to give it to – see if they can name that person, etc. Ensure that learners have every opportunity to do this entirely by themselves. Do not assume they can't do it and consequently deny them the opportunity to try for themselves. If learners can use language this should be incorporated into the routine. You can say, for example, 'John, could you ask Josh if he wants a turn.' Josh is encouraged to signal/answer 'Yes' or 'No' and so on.

Consider

Learners should always be given the option to signal or say that they don't want a turn. Being able to say 'No' is important. It empowers learners and builds trust.

Key: ✳︎ ▢ ⊙

Shaker, Shaker

Items required

Home-made shakers. Use plastic bottles – all shapes and sizes. I cover mine with holographic wrapping paper and seal by wrapping sticky tape around them until they are completely covered. This is a bit tricky but worth the effort in terms of longevity. These shakers are then put in a colourful or interesting bag.

Activity

Each person chooses a shaker from the bag to a verbal cue 'Take one'. Alternatively, offer a choice so that learners can choose by eye-pointing, reaching, etc. With an accompanying song, shake the shakers. Depending on the ability of learners this can lead to a variation of actions. For example, 'Shake it on your [body part]', 'Shake it [use prepositions]', 'Shake it [loudly, quietly or fast and slow]', etc. Adults can model. Finish the activity by collecting the shakers. Enable learners as you do so to put them in the bag. Use the verbal cue 'In the bag'.

Consider

Ask able learners to give out shakers (one-to-one correspondence) and collect at the end. Encourage learners to use appropriate language wherever possible and always leave enough time to enable learners' word-finding.

Key:

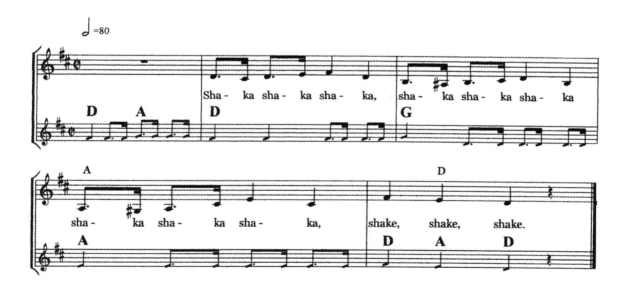

Sunshine Drum

Item required
A home-made drum. Mine is a strong, round plastic box filled with dried peas. I have used yellow holographic sticky-back plastic to create a large sun and rays on the top of the drum.

Activity
The song supports exploration/playing. It can be used in turn-taking routines to practise 'give and take'. Ask individuals if they want a turn. Encourage a reach gesture, vocalisation or language response, etc.

Consider
The facilitator, when developing the use of prepositions, can use activity items such as this: after each individual has had a turn the facilitator asks for the drum back; he or she then hides the drum/activity item and asks the next person 'Where's the drum?' and so on.

The tune of this song can also be used as a 'Hello'. 'Bring a little sunshine into our life and say hello to . . . say hello, say hello say hello to . . . '

Key:

Sunshine Drum

Shaker Up and Down

Item required
A survival blanket. I usually buy mine in a camping shop.

Activity
The facilitator goes into the inner circle and shakes the blanket up and down in front of a specific learner in order to encourage the learner to track it up and down. The qualities of a survival blanket enable it to be held up in the air long enough for learners to orientate their eyes upwards. Sing to the tune of 'John Brown's Body': 'Shaker shaker, shaker shaker up and down, shaker shaker, shaker shaker up and down, shaker shaker, shaker shaker up and down. Now put it over [name] 123.' The blanket then, in conjunction with the song, is placed over the head of the learner. Any kind of peek-a-boo style games can be incorporated, particularly if initiated by a learner. Ensure each learner gets a turn.

Consider
During the song leave pauses for learners to fill, either with a physical gesture or the words 'Up and down'. 'Shaker, shaker, shaker, shaker (pause) and (pause), etc.'

Key: ✳ ◇ ☺

Sunshine Ring

Item required
A sunshine ring. I made mine by threading together lots of yellow plastic lids (aerosol type) and then tying them into a ring.

Activity
This song supports exploration. The facilitator can control the 'give and take' here so that, before each person takes their turn, learners, if able, have to say where the ring is (prepositions). For example, 'Under the chair' or 'On the guitar'. A vocal addition can be added to the end of each verse to extend the exploration time: repeat tune but change words to: 'Do doobe do, do doobe do. Doobe doobe do do. Doo doobe do, do doobe do, doobe doobe do do.'

Consider
The sunshine ring makes a nice clatter sound – brilliant for exploration. Mine is tied together with a ribbon using kite material. This has proved helpful when learners enjoy throwing things because a helper can hold on to the ribbon while ensuring that experimental play and exploration with the lids remain with the learner. Here also is an opportunity to establish a game routine 'There it goes – here it comes.'

Key: ◑ ✳ ◉

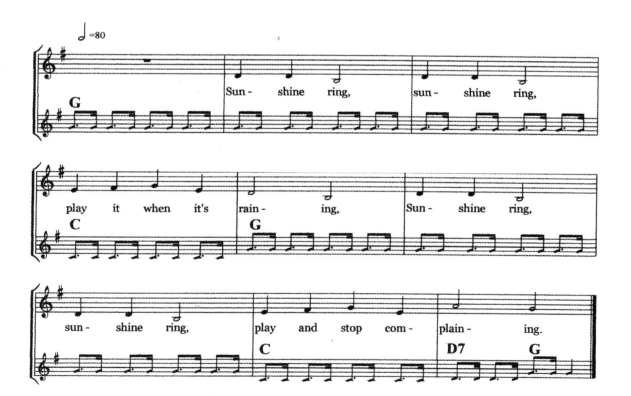

Time to Have Some Fun Today

Item required

Material: a silk sarong is perfect. Any colour will do but ensure it has a slightly see-through quality.

Activity

The facilitator holds the cloth at both ends and, moving around the inner circle, wafts it up and down while singing the song. To the tune of 'Pop Goes the Weasel' sing 'Time to have some fun today, time for smiles and laughter, time to have surprises too . . . uh oh [pause for an expectant reaction], I've got you' (the cloth goes over the learner). You may then sing 'Where is John', etc. in order to encourage them to pull it off. When they manage to do so, everyone acknowledges it, with either a vocal exclamation or a short phrase 'Here he is.'

Consider

During the pause a learner, with the help of the facilitator's expectant behaviour, says 'Uh oh' before the cloth reward is delivered.

This is a good activity to encourage peer interaction. Here, a learner goes into the middle and takes the lead. This means they have to get the timing approximately right, choose a person to go under the cloth, put it over their head and wait for the person to take it off. They can also sing the 'Where is . . . ' or perhaps just say the name of the person hiding under the cloth.

A learner may need to learn each stage of the activity. Along the way celebrate and positively reinforce any approximations.

Key: ○ ✳ ◇ ◻ ☺

Tiddley Um Pum Pum

Item required

A bodhrun drum or large tambour.

Activity

The facilitator moves around the inner circle singing the song and banging the drum in rhythmic fashion. As learners pay attention the facilitator or helper moves towards them and enables an individual learner to play, bang, touch the drum. The drum can be held in a supportive way, but ensure that learners are enabled to explore and play in whatever manner they choose. Continue the activity until all the learners have had a turn. Use your improvisational skills and sing about what the person is doing: 'Bang the drum' or 'Feel the drum' or 'Touch the drum', etc. The duration of a learner's turn depends very much on individual participation.

Consider

Holding a learner's hand (hand over hand) and banging it on a drum is rarely helpful; instead, a learner's hand (with that person's permission) can be placed on the drum. The drum is then moved up and down in order to create for that person a sense of what playing the drum is like.

Key: ◖ ✳ ◉

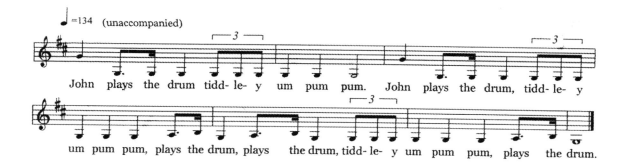

Bibliography

Alvin, J. (1974) 'The nature and scope of music therapy with handicapped children'. Paper read at the conferences held in Manchester and Birmingham. Herts: British Society for Music Therapy.

Berk, L. S. (1989) 'Neuroendocrine and stress hormone changes during mirthful laughter', *American Journal of Medical Science*, **298**(6), 390–6.

Bowlby, J. (1969) *Attachment and Loss, Vol. 1: Attachment*. London: Hogarth.

Bromwich, R. M. (1981) *Working with Parents and Infants: An Interactional Approach*. Baltimore: University Park Press.

Bulto, L. (1985) *Developmental Groupwork with Adolescents*. London: Hodder and Stoughton.

Bunt, L. (1994) *Music Therapy: An Art Beyond Words*. London: Routledge.

Burns, S. and Lamont, G. (1993) *Values and Vision*. London: Hodder and Stoughton.

Button, L. (1985) *Developmental Groupwork*. London: Hodder and Stoughton.

Caroe, L. L. (1995) 'Music and language: an investigation into how a variety of musical activities influence, support and contribute to young children's developing language'. Unpublished BA (Hons) enquiry, University of Brighton.

Christie, P. and Wimpory, D. (1986) 'Recent research into the development of communicative competence and its implications for the teaching of autistic children', *Communication*, **20**(1), 4–7.

Clough, P. (1998) 'Balancing acts: policy agenda for teacher education and special educational needs', *Journal of Education for Teaching*, **24**(1), 61–3.

Collis, M. and Lacey, P. (1996) *Interactive Approaches to Teaching: A Framework for INSET*. London: David Fulton.

Corke, M. (1999) 'Interactive Music: its nature and relevance to the social development of children with complex and multiple learning difficulties'. Unpublished BA (Hons) extended essay, University of Brighton.

Corke, M. and Turner, S. (1995/6) 'Developing Interactive Music'. Unpublished pilot study, no availability.

Coupe, J. and Goldbart, J. (1992) *Communication Before Speech*. London: Chapman and Hall.

Craig, W. (2000) *Childhood Social Development*. Oxford: Blackwell.

Davenport, G. C. (1988) *An Introduction to Child Development*. London: Unwin Hyman Ltd.

Davis, J. (2001) *A Sensory Approach to the Curriculum*. London: David Fulton.

DfEE (1997) *Excellence for All Children: Meeting Special Educational Needs* (CM 3785). London: HMSO.

Donaldson, M. (1986) *Children's Minds*. London: Fontana.

Dunn, J. (1988) *The Beginnings of Social Understanding*. Oxford: Blackwell.

Education Reform Act (1988) London: HMSO.

Ekman, P. (1989) *Charles Darwin: The Expression of the Emotions in Man and Animals* (3rd edition). London: HarperCollins.

Fisher, R. (1990) *Teaching Children to Think*. Oxford: Blackwell.

Fogel, A. (1979) 'Peer vs mother directed behaviour in 1–3-month-old infants', *Infant Behaviour and Development*, **2**, 215–26.

Fontana, D. (1995) *Psychology for Teachers* (3rd edition). London: Macmillan Press Ltd.

Forsyth, D. R. (1999) *Group Dynamics* (3rd edition). New York: Wadsworth Publishing Company.

Gardener, H. (1993) *Multiple Intelligences*. New York: Basic Books, a division of Harper-Collins.

Gleason, J. B. (1989) *The Development of Language* (3rd edition). New York: Macmillan Publishing Company.

Gray, D. E. and Denicolo, P. (1998) 'Research in special needs education: objectivity or ideology?', *British Journal of Special Education*, **25**(3), 140–5.

Greenspan, S. I. (1991) *Infancy and Early Childhood: The Practice of Clinical Assessment and Intervention with Emotional and Developmental Challenges*. Madison, CT: International University Press.

Gross, R. D. (1987) *Psychology: The Science of Mind and Behaviour*. London: Edward Arnold.

Gross, R. D. and McIlveen, R. (1998) *Psychology: A New Introduction*. London: Hodder and Stoughton.

Hargie, O., Saunders, C. and Dickson, D. (1994) *Social Skills in Interpersonal Communication*. London: Routledge.

Harris, P. C. (1989) *Children and Emotion*. Oxford: Basil Blackwell Ltd.

Hewett, D. and Nind, M. (eds) (1998) *Interaction in Action*. London: David Fulton.

Hicks, F. (1995) 'The role of music therapy in the care of the new born', *Nursing Times*, **91**(38), 31–3.

Kohut, H. (1977) *The Restoration of the Self*. New York: International University Press.

Kuhl, P. K. and Meltzoff, A. N. (1997) 'Evolution, nativism and learning in the development of language and speech', in Gopnik, M. (ed.) *The Inheritance and Innateness of Grammars*. New York: Oxford University Press.

Lacan, J. (1977) *Ecrits*. New York: Norton.

Longhorn, F. (1998) *A Sensory Curriculum for Very Special People*. London: Souvenir Press Ltd.

Longhorn, F. (2000) 'Multisensory education and learners with profound autism', in Powell, S. (ed.) *Helping Children with Autism to Learn*. London: David Fulton.

Lowis, M. J. (1998) 'Music and peak experiences: an empirical study', *The Mankind Quarterly*, **39**(2), Winter.

Lowis, M. J. and Nieuwoudt, J. M. (1993) 'The humor phenomenon: a theoretical perspective', *The Mankind Quarterly*, **32**(4), Summer.

Mahler, M. S. and Furer, M. (1968) *On Human Symbiosis and the Vicissitudes of Individuation*. New York: Basic Books.

McCall, R. B. and McGhee, P. E. (1997) 'The discrepancy hypothesis of attention and affect in infants', in Uzgiris, I. C. and Weizmann, F. (eds) *The Structuring of Experience.* New York: Plenum.

McConkey, R. and Price, P. (1986) *Let's Talk.* London: Souvenir Press.

McGhee, P. E. (1979) *Humor: Its Origins and Development.* New York: W. H. Freeman and Company.

McGhee, P. E. and Chapman, A. J. (eds) (1980) *Children's Humour.* New York: John Wiley and Sons Ltd.

McLinden, M. (1995) 'Touching the moon', *British Journal of Special Education,* **22**(22), 64–9.

Money, D. (1997) 'A comparison of three approaches to deliver a speech and language therapy service to people with learning difficulties', *European Journal of Disorders of Communication,* **32**, 446–9.

Murray, E. J. (1964) *Motivation and Emotion.* New Jersey: Prentice Hall Inc.

NACCCE Report (1999) 'All our futures: creativity, culture and education'. London: DfEE Publications.

Nind, M. (1996) 'Efficacy of intensive interaction: developing sociability and communication in people with severe and complex learning difficulties using an approach based on caregiver–infant interaction', *European Journal of Special Needs Education,* **11**(1), 48–66.

Nind, M. (1999) 'Intensive interaction and autism: a useful approach?', *British Journal of Special Education,* **26**(2), 96–102.

Nind, M. (2000a) 'Intensive interaction and children with autism', in Powell, S. (ed) *Helping Children with Autism to Learn.* London: David Fulton.

Nind, M. (2000b) 'Teachers' understanding of interactive approaches in special education', *International Journal of Disability, Development and Education,* **47**(2).

Nind M. and Hewett, D. (1994) *Access to Communication.* London: David Fulton.

Nordoff, P. and Robins, C. (1992) *Therapy in Music for Handicapped Children.* London: Victor Gollancz Ltd.

O'Donohue, J. (1999) *Anam Cara – Spiritual Wisdom from the Celtic World.* London: Bantam Books.

Olds, C. (1985) 'Fetal response to music', *Midwives Chronicle,* **98**(1170), 202–3.

Overton-Healy, J. (1995) 'Learning enhancement: utilizing effective teacher communication behaviours', *Educational Practice and Theory,* **17**(2), 71–5.

Pease, A. (1993) *Body Language.* London: Sheldon Press.

Piaget, J. (1952) *The Origins of Intelligence in Children.* New York: International Universities Press.

Preveezer, W. (1991) 'Musical interaction', *Speech and Language Disorders Newsletter,* **37**, 10–11.

Preveezer, W. (1993) *Developing Communication Through Music.* Training Course, 13 May, Meath Training, Meath School, Surrey.

Preveezer, W. (2000) 'Musical interaction and children with autism', in Powell, S. (ed.) *Helping Children with Autism to Learn.* London: David Fulton.

Priestley, J. G. (1992) 'Whitehead revisited – religion and education: an organic whole', in Watson, B. (ed.) *Priorities in Religious Education: A Model for the 1990s and Beyond.* London: Falmer Press.

Rae Smith, B. and Leinonen, E. (1992) *Clinical Pragmatics*. London: Chapman and Hall.

Robinson, P. (1996) (May) *Music and the Mind*. Channel Four television series.

Rogers, C. R. (1961) *On Becoming a Person: A Therapy View of Psychotherapy*. London: Constable.

Rogers, C. R. (1983) *Freedom to Learn for the Eighties*. Columbus, OH: Charles Merrill Publishers.

Rogers, C. R. (1986) 'A client centred/person centred approach to therapy', in Kutash, I. L. and Wolf, A. (eds) *Psychotherapist's Casebook*, 197–208. San Francisco: Jossey-Bass.

Rogers, C. R. (1990) *Client Centred Therapy*. London: Constable.

SCAA (1995) 'Spiritual and moral development', *SCAA Discussion Papers* (No. 3). London: SCAA.

Schaffer, D. and Dunn, J. (1979) *The First Year of Life*. New York: John Wiley and Sons Ltd.

Schaffer, H. R. (1971) *The Growth of Sociability*. Harmondsworth: Penguin.

Schaffer, H. R. (1977a) 'Early interactive development', in Schaffer, H. R. (ed.) *Studies in Mother–Infant Interaction*. London: Academic Press.

Schaffer, H. R. (1977b) *Studies in Mother–Infant Interaction*. London: Academic Press.

Schaffer, H. R. (1998) *Social Development*. Oxford: Blackwell.

Shaw, M. E. (1981) *Group Dynamics: The Psychology of Small Group Behaviour*. New York: McGraw-Hill.

Stern, D. (1977) *The First Relationship: Infant and Mother*. London: Fontana/Open Books.

Stern, D. N. (1985) *The Interpersonal World of The Infant*. New York: Basic Books.

Stone, M. K. (1995) *Don't Just Do Something: Sit There*. Norwich: Religious and Moral Education Press.

Storr, A. (1992) *Music and the Mind*. London: HarperCollins.

Stothard, V. (1998) 'The gradual development of intensive interaction in a school setting', in Hewett, D. and Nind, M. (eds) *Interaction in Action*. London: David Fulton.

Strickland, D. (1993) 'Seriously, laughter matters', *Today's O.R. Nurse*, November/December, 19–24.

Strongman, K. T. (1993) *The Psychology of Emotion*. New York: John Wiley and Sons Ltd.

Thorne, B. (1995) *Carl Rogers*. London: Sage Publications Inc.

Vygotsky, L. S. (1962) *Thought and Language*. New York: MIT Press.

Vygotsky, L. S. (1978) *Mind in Society: The Development of Higher Psychological Processes*. Cambridge, MA: Harvard University Press.

Wadsworth, B. J. (1984) *Piaget's Theory of Cognition and Affective Development*. New York: Longman Inc.

Watson, J. and Knight, C. (1991) 'An evaluation of Intensive Interaction with pupils with severe learning difficulties', *Child Language Teaching and Therapy*, **7**, 310–25.

Wells, G. C. (1981) *Learning Through Interaction*. Cambridge: Cambridge University Press.

Wells, G. C. (1992) *The Meaning Makers*. London: Heinemann Educational Books.

Wester, W. C. and O'Grady, D. J. (1991) *Hypnosis with Children*. New York: Bruner Matel.

Whitebread, D. (ed.) (2000) *The Psychology of Teaching and Learning in Primary School*. London: Routledge/Falmer.

Wimpory, D. (1985) *Enabling Communication in Young Autistic Children*. Video, available from Child Development Research Unit, Nottingham University.

Wimpory, D. C. (1995a) 'Brief report: musical interaction therapy for children with autism. An evaluative case study with two year follow up', *Journal of Autism and Developmental Disorder,* **25**(5), 541–52.

Wimpory, D. C. (1995b) 'Social engagement in preschool children with autism'. Unpublished Doctoral Thesis, University of Wales, Bangor, Gwynedd.

Wimpory, D. C. (1999) 'Musical interaction therapy for children with autism', in Schaffer, C. (ed.) *Innovative Psychotherapy Techniques in Child and Adolescent Therapy.* New York: John Wiley and Sons, Inc.

Wimpory, D. C. and Nash, S. (1999) 'Musical interaction therapy – therapeutic play for children with autism', *Child Teaching and Therapy,* **5**, 17–28.

Wood, D. (1992) *How Children Think and Learn.* Oxford: Blackwell.

Wood, D. (1998) *How Children Think and Learn* (2nd edition). Oxford: Blackwell.

Wood, M. E. (1973) *Children: The Development of Personality and Behaviour.* London: George G. Harrap and Co. Ltd.

Wright, H. (1987) *Groupwork Perspectives and Practice.* London: Scutan Press.

Index